Kathy Sue Loudermilk, I Love You

Lewis Grizzard

 Peachtree Publishers, Ltd.

Published by
PEACHTREE PUBLISHERS, LTD.
494 Armour Circle, N.E., Atlanta, Georgia 30324

Manufactured in the United States of America

Text design by David Russell
Cover design by Joan Stoliar

Library of Congress Cataloging in Publication Data

Grizzard, Lewis, 1946–
    Kathy Sue Loudermilk, I love you.

      I.   Title.
AC8.G948   081   79-22309
ISBN 0-931948-05-3

To
Christine and H. B.

Contents

Foreword

Lewis Grizzard asked me to write the foreword to this book. I'm flattered, because Lewis is one of my favorite people.

Also, he saved my marriage, perhaps even the roof over my head. I will explain. I will begin at the beginning, when I personally discovered Lewis Grizzard.

It was 1968, when I was executive sports editor of The *Atlanta Journal*. We needed to hire a beginning sports writer, and I went about finding one in my usual scientific way.

I went to a certain coach, whom I knew to be paranoid, ill-tempered and, on occasion, inclined to lie. "Coach," I said, "who is the worst young sports writer you know?"

"Lewis Grizzard," he replied, "that jerk who works for the *Athens Daily News*."

I hired Lewis that very afternoon.

He was an instant hit in the sports department. Being from Moreland, Georgia, he talked like people are supposed to and he understood the importance of getting the Friday night wrestling results into the Saturday paper.

He was twenty-one years old, had a pretty blonde wife, a worn-out Volkswagon, and he did everything I told him to do.

Lewis was on his way to becoming the best wrestling writer in Atlanta when our sports slot man quit.

In every sports department there is an individual called the "man who does the slot." It's just a sexy term for the one who does all the work while the rest of us cover the World Series and the Sugar Bowl.

The slot man comes to work at four in the morning and sometimes works until two the next morning. But he doesn't have to worry about filling out an overtime slip because he qualifies as a supervisor.

That's the job I had fallen into shortly after Grizzard came aboard. My wife had not seen me fully awake in three months and my children actually thought I was deceased.

My wife called the office one midnight and made it fairly clear: "Get somebody to do the slot or get a lawyer," she said.

"Lewis," I said. "How would you like to do the slot?"

"Remember," I said, "you get a $5 raise and Saturday off."

I didn't explain that I meant every third Saturday in July. Grizzard took the job. Three months later his wife divorced him.

One day I took Lewis out for a beer. "Kid," I said, "you've got a great future in this business. What do you really want to do with your life?"

"Someday, I want to have my own barbecue place," he answered. "With sliced pork pig sandwiches and cold beer in long-neck bottles. With a jar of pickled pigs feet next to the cash register and an ol' hound dog next to me. Most afternoons I would close up and go fishing, and some afternoons I would even put bait on the hook."

I knew Lewis was a comer. When I somehow became managing editor of The *Atlanta Constitution,* Lewis got my old job as executive sports editor of The *Journal,* the youngest ever. He moved on to become associate city editor at The *Journal,* and special assignments editor at The *Constitution.*

Later (I forget the details) he wound up sports editor of the *Chicago Sun-Times.*

I went up there to visit him once. He took me out to lunch, and the wind was so strong they had a *rope* you had to hold onto walking from the newspaper to the restaurant. We had to write out our order because the waitress couldn't understand us. Stray dogs in Moreland might not have eaten what they served us.

After about two years in Chicago, Lewis started calling me every night. Collect.

"I'm looking out my window," he'd say, "watching a guy mug a little old lady."

Or, "Thirty-third day in a row below zero."

Or, "Just had another bowl of boiled Polish cabbage."

He was down to 124 pounds and having fainting spells.

One night I casually mentioned I was trying to hire a columnist for The *Constitution*.

"Hire me!" Grizzard screamed.

Nevermind that he'd never written a newspaper column.

Nevermind that he's already quit the Atlanta papers about six times.

If they can't take a joke, to hell with 'em, I decided.

Besides, the long-distance charges were getting impossible to explain.

So Grizzard came back to Atlanta to write a column for The *Constitution*.

He's up to 189 pounds, and if you think you'll ever catch him in the office you're kidding yourself.

He's the hottest thing on Southern newsprint.

Everywhere I go people ask me if I know Lewis Grizzard.

"Do you ever get to talk to him?" they ask.

"No," I reply. "But one day on the elevator he nodded to me."

And one day he did.

Jim Minter
Managing Editor
The *Atlanta Journal*

• 1 •

COMING HOME IS A ONE-WAY TRIP

I lived in Chicago for two years before returning to Atlanta to begin writing a daily column for The Atlanta Constitution. Chicago's not a bad town. But the weather didn't suit me, and the food didn't suit me, and people talked funny.

When I lived in Chicago, I used to think of the line from the country song that went, "If I ever get back to Georgia, I'm gonna nail my feet to the ground." What the following columns about home and where my heart is should say is, I finally got back to Georgia and I'll be dipped in hot buttered grits before I'll leave again.

CHICAGO — What this neighborhood must have been fifty years ago! Eight blocks north on Lincoln Avenue is the Biograph Theatre where they shot John Dillinger down. The Biograph lives on with nostalgia flicks. Bogart and Davis in *Petrified Forest* for $1.50. Four blocks north on Clark Street is the site of the Saint Valentine's day Massacre, now the site of a home for old people who don't have homes. Capone, I am told, operated south. This was Bugs Moran's territory.

Today, it is ethnic and Democratic, congested and overpriced. It is alternately charming and frustrating. An automobile is an albatross. There is no place to park it. But this has been home for two years, and these are the very last moments.

The dwarfish old man who delivers for the liquor store on the corner has already made two runs on my street, and it's barely ten o'clock. Bloody Mary mix mostly. Bloody Marys are big anywhere on Sunday mornings. On the near north side of Chicago, they are a way of life.

The line is already forming for brunch at R. J. Grunts. For $3.50—fork in one hand, plate in the other—you can shovel through a cornucopia somebody grossly underestimated and called a salad bar. Hash browns are extra with the eggs. Hash browns are a bad joke Chicago restaurants play on breakfast.

The Loop is only ten minutes away. The most poignant memory will be the bleak, snowy afternoon a fire department ambulance, followed by four black limousines and a cadre of policemen on motorcycles, drove solemnly up Michigan Avenue, past the Wrigley Building and across the river, while all the power and force that is Chicago commerce came to a reverent halt. Inside the ambulance rode the corpse of Richard J. Daley.

Lake Michigan and the endless high rises on Lakeshore Drive's gold coast are just across Lincoln Park where, on days that weather permits, thousands flock to walk on something that is not asphalt

3

or concrete. It is warm this morning, and thank God for that. Chicago has two seasons, they like to say: Winter and the Fourth of July.

Songs and poems are written about saying goodbye because it is one of those things in life that is usually impossible to do gracefully if it is worth doing at all. I got mine out of the way a day early. "If you're ever in Atlanta. . . ."

Slowly, a final order does come to the mess that is necessary for the moving of all one's earthly belongings. My plane is at noon. There is one last run through the back bedrooms, and the movers left a box. Anybody need a dart board, a rickety lawn chair, and forty-five slightly-used tennis balls?

The cab pulls out on North Cleveland, left to Fullerton, and on to the Kennedy Expressway where it's every man for himself to O'Hare. Some of it I have liked a great deal. Some of it I may have even loved. There were parts I hated. Regardless. It's over.

****

Living in a city other than Atlanta was something I had never considered. I am not native, but close. And Atlanta—even when the Dinkler Plaza was the big stop and Terminal Station was busy at midnight—was a mecca for those of us in the Coweta County hinterlands. "Atlaner" they called it where I lived, and a lot of people went there on Friday nights. Those who didn't stop at the Farmers' Market drove on to the city auditorium for the wrestling matches. No, the *rasslin'* matches.

Predictably, my first job out of school was in Atlanta. The changes were already at hand. Up jumped the Stadium and in came the Braves, the Falcons, the Hawks, and the Flames. Underground flourished and the *New York Times* did front page stories. Bobby Dodd retired, Lester Maddox faded, and Hartsfield went international. And everybody from Keokuk and Three Rivers showed up in his leisure suit for the hardware convention at the Marriott or the Regency. The Nitery? One block up and two over.

I left Atlanta two years ago for Chicago, figuring what the hell, horizons are for stretching. I was homesick at the first stop light in Cartersville. Horizons without a red clay motif are somebody else's horizons.

I did keep up while I was gone. Jimmy Carter, a Georgian, became president, and that helped. Suddenly, it was fashionable at Hotspurs and Arnie's in Chicago to be able to explain the difference between poke salet and pot likker. A man stood on the corner of Rush and State and called another a "sumbitch." I swear.

Time Magazine even devoted a special issue to explaining the South. I noted with no small measure of pride that it no longer considered H. L. Mencken's dismissal of the cultural South as the "intellectual Gobi or Lapland" to be operative.

Ted Turner was front page in Chicago. "Is he a little goofy?" I was asked more than once. Midwesterners can't really distinguish between Georgia Tech and just plain Georgia, but when Pepper upset Notre Dame last fall the question did come up. *Playboy* said the women were great in Atlanta. *Sports Illustrated* said the sports teams were lousy. Could be worse, I said. What if it were the other way around?

I am sure a lot has changed. The new hotels are supposed to be incredible. One allegedly has a lake in the lobby. It is rumored liquor may be purchased on Sunday. Parts of the city, I understand, have disappeared altogether in the wake of MARTA bulldozers. And Mr. Young has gone to New York and Mr. Fowler has gone to Washington in his place.

But folks still talk nice to you, don't they? And Harold's Barbecue hasn't closed? Northside Drive from the expressway to West Paces has not gone commercial? And late on summer afternoons what of that stillness, that cooling, that sundown in the Deep South that makes whatever happened during the day worth it and whatever may transpire that night even better? Has the Fox been saved?

I hope so. The commitment is made.

The Delta lady on the other end of the phone was talking. "There is space available on the noon flight to Atlanta," she said a few days ago. "Will this be round trip?"

I just let it hang there, savoring the moment.

"No, m'am," I answered. "One way."

No Spot Is So Dear . . .

On a cold day last week, I stood outside the church in my hometown of Moreland, Georgia, that is so dear to my childhood and tried to remember how long it had been since I was inside. Ten years? At least that long. But if there weren't still roots here, would I come back so often in my mind?

Church was about all we had. Sunday school was at ten, but preaching was only twice a month. We shared sermons and the preacher with another flock down the road.

What did they call it on Sunday night? MYF? We had a couple of rowdy brothers in town who broke into a store. They were juvenile first offenders. Their punishment was to attend Methodist Youth Fellowship for six months. First night they were there, they beat up two fifth-graders and threw a Cokesbury hymnal at the lady who met with us and always brought cookies.

She ducked in time and then looked them squarely in their devilish eyes. Soft as the angel she was, she said, "I don't approve of what you boys did here tonight, and neither does Jesus. But if He can forgive you, I guess I'll have to."

She handed them a plate of cookies, and last I heard, both are daddies with steady jobs and rarely miss a Sunday. That was the first miracle I ever saw.

Revivals at the church were the highlight of the summer. I remember a young visiting preacher talking about the night he was converted.

"I was drunk in an Atlanta bar," he said, "and I was lost. But Jesus walked in and sat down beside me. Praise His name, because that's the reason I'm with you here tonight."

That frightened me. If Jesus could find that fellow in an Atlanta bar, he certainly wouldn't have any trouble walking up on me smoking behind the pump house in Moreland. I always took an extra look around before lighting up after that.

Workers were smoking one day in the attic of our church. They left a cigarette. It took less than an hour for flames to destroy that old building. I didn't cry, but grown men did.

We built it back—of brick this time. Country folks will dig deep in the name of the Lord.

The best fried chicken I ever ate, the best iced tea I ever drank were the fried chicken and the iced tea on Homecoming Day at the church. Dinner on the grounds, we called it. The chickens had been walking in someone's backyard earlier in the morning. The tea went into a galvanized washtub. A piece of block ice kept it cold.

The day Red Murphy died, they announced it in the church. The congregation wept as one. Everyone loved Red Murphy. He ran the little post office and took children on pony rides.

Maxine Estes taught my Sunday school class. In rural Georgia in the fifties, she was big on being kind to your neighbor no matter the color of his skin. I learned to sing Hymn No. 153, "Love, Mercy and Grace," in that church. And "What a Friend We Have in Jesus." And the one I still break into occasionally today, "Precious Memories." They do linger.

My mother married my stepfather inside that church. And one hot Saturday afternoon a long time ago, a pretty nineteen-year-old girl married me at the same altar. I told her I would never forget her, and I haven't.

It's easy to fall away from the church, no matter the closeness to it in times past. I have done it. So have you. Grown people can do as they please. The 10:30 Sunday morning movie is even an excuse I use. So are Saturday nights that should have ended a lot earlier.

I never could bring myself to walk inside my old church last week. But some Sunday morning soon, maybe I will. And maybe I'll put a ten in the collection plate, and maybe they'll have chicken and iced tea, and maybe afterward I'll make a habit of it.

There is a new country song out. An old man is singing to a group of fellow derelicts. "Lean on Jesus," goes the chorus, "before He leans on you."

I'm not one to panic, but it's something to think about.

Country Store

There is no sign, but the lady inside at Bailey's General Store assured me this was, in fact, Jones Crossroads.

"The Joneses don't own the land anymore," she said, "but they still call it 'Jones Crossroads.' " Who's being picky?

Jones Crossroads is one country store and a house or two and some nice trees at the intersection of Georgia highways 18 and 219 half the distance between West Point and Pine Mountain. The population depends on how many people needed to go to the store that day.

I have a thing about country stores, a love affair that goes back to my youth and a wonderful place called Cureton and Cole's. I could never quite understand why Cureton and Cole's was owned by Lee Evans and J. W. Thompson, but again, who's being picky?

You name it, they sold it at Cureton and Cole's in downtown Moreland, as long as it was coal, sacks of guano, corn meal, Sugar Daddy all day suckers, Hollywood candy bars, Zero candy bars, Zagnut candy bars, snuff, work shirts, work pants, work shoes, kerosene, soda crackers, Vienna sausage, Home Run cigarettes, potatoes—sweet and Irish—Blue Horse notebook paper, ice cream in cups with lids that if you licked the ice cream off the underside you would uncover the picture of a movie star like Yvonne DeCarlo, Prince Albert in a can, chicken feed, thread, seed, moon pies, and cold drinks such as R.C. Colas, Nehi oranges, Double Colas, and NuGrapes from a box filled with chunks of block ice, and other of life's necessities.

Sadly, Cureton and Cole's has been boarded shut, never to open again. At least they haven't torn it down and put up a disco. I can see it now: J. W.'s Juke Joint.

Bailey's General Store in Jones Crossroads is a lot like Cureton and Cole's. It has a front porch and two chairs for just sittin'. It has a screened front door and a thermometer so old men can look at it and greet one another with, "Hot enough for you?"

Inside, there are hardwood floors and an air-conditioning system

—a floor fan. I saw some flies. A fly is never at home until it is buzzing about a country store on a hot afternoon.

The lady inside said her daddy, Mr. Bailey, ran the store before he died. Worked hard all his life, she said, until the day he found out he had cancer. He lived five more weeks.

"Daddy did a lot of business here," she said. "Mama took it over after he died. Things have sort of gone down hill since then."

I checked out the merchandise. In the back were sacks of hog pellets and scratch feed for chickens. There was a meat box with bologna, the kind you cut directly from the loaf. A yard rake was for sale.

There was a classic candy display case. Zagnut must be out of business. Behind the counter was more snuff than your grandmother could dip in a lifetime of evenings in the front porch rocking chair. There was Bruton's snuff, and Dental snuff, and Tops snuff, and I think I spotted a can of Rooster.

I couldn't resist any longer. From inside Bailey's drink box I pulled out a Nehi orange bellywasher. From the cookie and cracker rack I plucked a "Big Town" chocolate moon pie.

I walked outside and sat me down on the front porch. The marshmallow filling inside the moon pie had become runny from the heat, but the cold rush of the orange bellywasher released its hold from the roof of my mouth.

For a moment I had been ten again, with a dime burning a hole in my jeans, and with all the pleasures a child could imagine encircling me and dazzling me. For a moment, I thought I could hear Lee Evans talking to J. W. Thompson. For a moment, that moon pie was chateaubriand and my big orange was a gentle and soothing nectar of the gods.

It's Okay to Cry

Things my mother told me would come true when I was grown that I really didn't believe at the time:

The older you get, the harder it is to quit smoking.

You might turn up your nose at turnip greens now, but there will come a time you can't get them and you will want them more than T-bone steak.

Love is the greatest gift one person can give to another.

Money can't buy love.

The kind it might buy isn't worth having.

People will tell you they love you when they don't mean it.

There are no answers in the bottom of a cocktail glass.

It's easy to go into debt. Getting out is next to impossible.

Marriage is a two-way street.

You will never meet a good woman in a night club.

One lie begets another.

If you don't take care of yourself when you are young, you might not live to regret it.

Even if you don't agree with everything the preacher says, it won't hurt you to sit still for thirty minutes and listen to him.

It's okay to cry.

Never let a friend down. You will need him someday.

You don't need to talk dirty to prove you are a man.

The Lord listens to your prayers.

He doesn't answer all of them.

The best way to tell somebody you care is to show them first.

It's not written anywhere that life is supposed to be fair.

Money doesn't grow on trees.

Always wear clean underwear. You might be in a wreck.

Children and old people appreciate kindness.

So do dogs.

Be careful when you buy a used car or an insurance policy.

Pay attention when somebody older tells you something. You can learn a lot from people who have already been down the road.

Being stubborn won't get you anywhere.

Women don't like men who drink too much.

There will be times when you are very lonely. Just remember your mother loves you and always will.

People who shout to make themselves heard usually don't know what they are talking about.

When you get older, your back will hurt and it won't be that easy to get to sleep.

Someday, a man will walk on the moon. And Pepsi Colas will cost a quarter.

Pretty faces can be deceiving.

Always say "Thank you" when somebody does you a favor. You will get more favors that way.

Ball games aren't the most important thing in the world.

Income tax will eat you alive.

You will regret not keeping up your piano lessons.

A Mother Will Worry

I have always disliked hospitals. They even smell like people are sick. And everybody who works there dresses all in white. That makes me uncomfortable, too.

Every moment I am visiting in a hospital, I expect one of those people in white to attempt to puncture my body with a needle. In medical science, when in doubt, grab a needle and look for a victim.

She was lying there in her hospital bed, asleep and attached to a strange looking machine. There was a needle in her arm. It was attached to a tube which led to a bottle of solution.

The solution, a drop at a time, rolled down to the tube, into the needle, and into her body. Each time a drop fell from the bottle, the machine made a clicking sound. The Chinese, I am certain, are behind such a torture-rendering machine.

I don't know what awakened her. Perhaps it was simply my presence in the room. I hadn't made a sound.

She looked tired. I have seen her like this so many times before. Once, when I was a child, she was sick and in the hospital for a long time. That was for something else, something she eventually whipped.

I am praying for an encore this time.

My mother first fell ill to her disease fifteen years ago. She went through a long, treacherous operation the day John Kennedy was buried.

She was better for a time after that, and then worse, and then better and then worse again. One day last week she said, "I haven't felt this good in years."

But it was no time before she was back in the hospital again and I was standing over her again, trying to say something that would help and instead talking mostly about myself.

One thing I never bring up to my mother is any involvement I might be having with the opposite sex, but she always asks about it because one thing she would like to be—like most mothers, I suppose—is a grandmother, and so far, she hasn't been close.

"There's plenty of time for that," I always tell her.

"Maybe for me," she laughs, "but how about you?"

The preacher came by. He was a soft man, who literally crept into the room and introduced himself to me by saying, "Hello, I'm a Baptist preacher."

He told my mother he was praying for her, and she thanked him. He didn't stay long.

"He goes by to see just about everybody," my mother explained. Visit the sick and calm the grieving. Nobody does it better than a small-town preacher.

I was there maybe a couple of hours. I finally pulled a chair near the bed toward the end of my visit. I think my mother sensed I would be leaving soon.

I am thirty-two years old. I have a good job. A car. A nice place to live. Friends. And more health than I deserve.

My mother is sick, lying in a hospital bed with a Chinese Solution Torture Machine attached to her arm. But here is how our visit ended:

"Are you eating well, son?"

"Sure."

"Remember to eat well. Sweets are bad for your teeth."

"I'll remember that."

"Don't ever pick up a stranger when you're driving at night."

"I would never do that."

"Do you have enough cover for your bed?"

"Plenty."

"I wish you would stop smoking."

"I've tried."

"Try harder."

"I'll try harder."

"Don't bother to get me anything for Christmas. I don't need a thing."

"I want to get you *something*."

"And don't worry about me."

"I can't help that."

"Do you have enough cover for your bed?"

"Plenty, mother. Plenty."

Mother's Day

She married late in life, compared to other women of her day. When she finally found her man, he would soon leave her and go off to war.

He was a brave soldier and performed many heroic deeds, and he lived through it all. When he returned, she loved him dearly and he loved her. A boy child was born one October morning.

But came another war that took her man away again.

She got the news from a yellow telegram. The child was playing in the yard, chasing butterflies and wrestling a playful bird dog. He can still remember her scream from within the house. He can still remember her tears. He was too young to understand why she was crying, but he tried to comfort her the best he could.

Her brave soldier, said the telegram, was missing in action. An enemy force had overrun his company's position on some barren hill a million miles away in Korea.

The child wondered about this "Korea," what it was, where it was, and why his daddy was there.

On Christmas Eve, there was a telephone call, followed by more tears. The soldier was alive. He was calling from a hospital in Pearl Harbor. He would be home soon.

"Do you still love me?" he asked his son.

The child did not yet understand the telephone. He nodded a "yes."

"Of course, he does," the mother assured the father. "And so do I."

He returned in triumph. He had been captured and imprisoned by the enemy. He had been tortured. But he had escaped. For weeks, he was hidden in an underground cave and cared for by a South Korean boy who brought him rice and kept him alive until he could make his way back to his lines.

He was weak from the diet and the fear. His feet were so severely frostbitten, they would crack open and bleed each day of the rest of his life.

He was a patriot, still. He made speeches throughout the land, his wife and son at his side. He told of his experiences and he assailed those who would keep American forces out of distant lands threatened by the spread of Communism.

He would say many times, "There is no soldier like the American soldier. The rest of the world *needs* us to keep it free."

But those many years of combat had taken their toll. He had changed. When he returned, the woman thought their long periods of separation were over. She would be disappointed again.

He brooded. He awakened nights in a cold sweat, screaming. He drank only a little at first. But then he would sit up those nights, alone with a bottle.

The Army, despite his many decorations for valor and his years of service, decided him unfit for further military duty. He wandered aimlessly, at a loss for a purpose.

The mother and the child would see him whenever they could. They would visit him in other cities and she would pretend someday they would be together again.

But she knew they wouldn't. A thousand nights, thinking the child next to her was asleep, she prayed aloud for help.

Finally, she gave up on her husband. She had no other choice.

He was a hopeless alcoholic, a man lost in an imagined shame that was nearly demonic in its possession of his life.

She educated herself. She struggled to work each day and to evening classes at night. Somehow, she still managed to bring her son toward manhood and she told him, "Always respect your father, no matter what."

She would eventually remarry. She would take a man steady and kind to her and to her son. She would find at least a share of the contentment and security that had avoided her for so long.

The father, the brave soldier, would die alone. The son would grow and leave her. But he would think of his mother and her plight often. On occasion, he would remember to thank her for the sacrifices she made in his behalf.

Sadly, her burdens have never ceased totally. Today, it is an illness she battles. The doctors say it is incurable. She *deserves* a miracle.

She wanted to be with her son today, and he wanted to be with her on Mother's Day. He wonders if he made the right decision to put off the visit because of business demands.

He did send roses, however. And because she means so much to him, and because she was strong on his mind, and because he wanted to remind himself of the long road she's been down, he spent an afternoon and half a night writing what you just read.

• 2 •

OFF THE WALL

People ask me, "Where do you get your ideas for columns?" I never know how to answer that question. Sometimes I look under rocks. I think that is where I got the ideas for the following pieces. At any rate, I do hate liver and I remain convinced the world would be better off without airplanes.

They Gave the Ball Without Me

For the thirty-second consecutive year, I did not receive an invitation to the annual Harvest Ball at the Piedmont Driving Club. Obviously, there has been some kind of mistake.

Every year, I anxiously await the arrival of the white envelope beckoning me to what is certainly one of Atlanta's most prestigious and gala social events.

And every year, I am disappointed. Could the problem be I have moved around too much and they don't know where to find me?

I could just drop by the club and pick it up, you know, and I promise to leave the truck on the street.

What happens at the Harvest Ball is some of the city's loveliest and tenderest and most charming young girlpersons, whose daddies also have a big stash, make their "debuts" to society.

That makes them "debutantes." I have never quite understood exactly what a debutante is, but I'm sure there are lots of good things to eat and drink at their parties.

"When a girl makes her debut," somebody who should know told me, "it means her parents are presenting her to their friends and that she is now a part of the social scene."

I think the male comparison to that—on a lower social strata—is your old man taking you for a beer at the VFW and letting you shoot pool with Scooter Haines who was once eight ball champion of all Heard County.

They held this year's Harvest Ball last week and, again, I had to be satisfied with reading about it in the paper.

It was a grand affair. Proud fathers, said the report, beamed as their daughters curtsied to the audience in their expensive and chic gowns.

One of the debs did express concern her escort might get too drunk to cut in on her father when it came time for the evening's waltz. That shocked me.

I can understand getting too drunk to shoot eight ball with Scooter Haines, but the Piedmont Driving Club ain't the Moose Lodge, sport.

Dinner was divine, the story went on. Everybody had tomato aspic with shrimp, breast of chicken, spinach souffle with artichokes and almond mousse and even Scooter Haines, who once went all the way to Houston for a pool tournament, never wrapped his gums around anything like that.

Sadly, the closest I have ever come to a debutante ball was the annual Fourth of July Street Dance in front of the knitting mill on the square in downtown Moreland with a live band that played "Down Yonder" over and over again because that's all the band knew except for "Alabama Jubilee" which it didn't play so well.

What always happened at the dance was farmers from as far away as Luthersville and Arno-Sargent showed up with truckloads of daughters they wanted to marry off. If any of them had teeth, they got to ride up front in the cab.

Some grand old girls got out of trucks at those street dances. The only curtseying they did, however, was over behind the depot where nobody could see them. We were a polite society, too.

There was Cordie Mae Poovey. Cordie Mae always came in her "bermudalls." That's a pair of overalls cut off just above the knee. Cordie Mae couldn't dance a lick, but don't tell her that because she weighed a good 220 and was stronger than she smelled.

And who could forget Lucille Garfield? Lucille carried her pet pig everywhere she went. The way you could tell the pig from

Lucille was the pig wore a hat and was the better conversationalist of the two.

Betty Jean Turnipseed didn't miss a dance for fifteen years. Betty Jean wasn't very smart. One time somebody brought an armadillo to school for show-and-tell and she thought it was a possum on the half-shell.

But Kathy Sue Loudermilk came to the street dances, too, and when she danced, even the preacher broke a sweat. Nature blessed 'that child beyond the limits of this timid vocabulary.

It's like my boyhood friend and idol, Weyman C. Wannamaker Jr., a great American, said of her: "That dog can hunt."

So I'll probably never make the Harvest Ball. But I would have paid to have seen Kathy Sue Loudermilk debuting at the Piedmont Driving Club.

One curtsey from ol' Kathy Sue in something tight and low cut and the whole crowd would have been knocked squarely on their tomato aspics.

Interviewing Myself

I get letters from journalism students and other assorted weirdos wanting to know how I go about putting together a column five days a week.

"I have to write a term paper for my JRL 101 class," began one recent letter, "and I have chosen you as my topic. I want to know, in at least 2,000 words, how you go about putting together a column five days a week.

"I need your response no later than two weeks from Friday. Please double-space and try to avoid typographical errors as the instructor counts off for that."

The student who wrote that letter will probably grow to be a good columnist. Getting other people to do your work is a cornerstone of this profession.

Since is is impossible for me to answer all such inquiries, I have decided today to interview myself on the subject of writing a column for the benefit of interested students and my boss.

I know my boss is interested because just the other day he asked me, "Grizzard, how can you do this to me five days a week?"

Here, then, is the interview, conducted in my office, which is located near the men's rest room and which recently got new carpet the color of river water near a chemical dump. I am using an IBM Selectric II typewriter which makes strange sounds like a semi hauling hogs through Holly Springs, Mississippi, on a hot July afternoon:

What does a semi hauling hogs through Holly Springs, Mississippi, on a hot, July afternoon sound like?"

"Grrrrrrrrrrroooooooooink!"

When your IBM Selectric II typewriter makes that sound, what do you think of?

The odor of overcrowded hogs in a steam bath and possible death by electrocution.

Has anybody ever suffered serious injury or even death in an accident involving an electric typewriter?

Yes. One day a skinny religion reporter got his tie hung in the paper roller of his electric typewriter. In a vain attempt to remove it, he rolled his head into his machine and was typed to death by a lower case 'j' and an out-of-control ampersand.

Do readers sometimes call and suggest column ideas to you?

Every day. Recently, an anonymous caller suggested I do a column on the most handsome, best-dressed sportscaster on Atlanta television.

Did you follow up on the suggestion?

Of course not. I knew it was Harmon the minute he mispronounced "Robert Hall."

As a columnist, do you have opportunities for exciting travel and adventure?

You betcha. Just in the last two months, I have been to Memphis and Birmingham. Memphis was closed after dark and under martial law, but the hotel in Birmingham had one of those neat, revolving restaurants like the Regency Hyatt in Atlanta. Unfortunately, the one in Birmingham was in the basement.

Last year, I got to go to the Indianapolis 500 automobile race. What an interesting event that was. It was the most mental illness I have seen at one time.

Approximately, what are your working hours?

I am on call twenty-four hours a day. No story is ever too big or too small for a good columnist. If the bartender forgot to tell you the office called, however, it's not your fault.

Who are the most difficult people to interview?

Those whose names recently appeared in the obituary column, anybody in Harrison's on Friday night with a wedding ring in his pocket, and Korean soccer players.

Is it a strain on your health to write five columns a week?

Absolutely not. I have migraine headaches, stomach pains, dizzy spells, nightmares, hallucinations, ingrown toenails, smoker's cough, and my back is stiff. Other than that, I am in perfect health for a sixty-five-year-old malaria victim.

It is necessary to drink to be a good columnist?

That is a common myth, but a young person setting out on a career as a columnist should avoid drinking at all costs. It is certainly not necessary to drink to be a good columnist. It is a great help on the days you are a bad one, however.

In summary, then, what is the most difficult part of writing a daily column: (a) the research; (b) the actual writing; (c) the need for a constant flow of the creative juices; or (d) crazies threatening to break your hands?

(E) Admitting to myself I can't hold down a regular job.

Liver Is a Fraud

Eating used to be so simple. A couple of eggs with grits, bacon, toast and coffee in the morning, a quick hamburger and fries at noon, and evening was your basic meat and potatoes.

Give me something with character in the evenings. A steak.

Pork chops. Fried chicken. My mother would occasionally try to slip liver into my diet.

"Eat liver, live longer," she would say.

I'm still taking my chances. Who wants a long life that includes eating liver? I don't even like to be in the same room with it.

After I left my mother's table, eating became a bit more complicated. Restaurant food can make eating more of a chore than a joy.

When I lived in Chicago, I nearly starved. Chicago is filled with ethnic restaurants that are fun once. But man can not live on a steady diet of veal marsala and things that still have their heads and eyes.

He must also have cornbread and collards and an occasional barbecue pork-pig sandwich. Otherwise, scurvy and rickets are distinct possibilities.

Today, eating has become a major problem. That is because all the things we used to think were good for us are actually bad for us. Like light bread and biscuits. Light bread and biscuits, somebody told me, are fattening, have no food value and can lead to heart attack and cancer. Say it ain't so.

The same goes for too much milk and eggs. They cause cholesterol and cholesterol causes your arteries to clog and clogged arteries are one-way tickets to the coronary wing.

You have probably heard bacon and hamburgers cause cancer. My doctor told me not to eat pork. That's a problem. A week without barbecue, and I hallucinate and get shortness of breath.

I was hoping they would find something wrong with liver. I always figured it probably caused the spread of communism if nothing else.

"Eat liver, live longer," said my doctor, the dirty pinko.

What we are supposed to be eating today are natural foods. Foods that have not been processed. Foods that have no chemical additives and preservatives. Foods that give us bulk and fibre.

All that sounds like good advice on how to keep your lawnmower engine in tune, but I decided to at least seek more information on the matter.

I have a friend who eats nothing but natural foods. Actually, he doesn't eat. He grazes. I went to him for advice.

"Breakfast," he said, "is the most important meal of the day. I eat natural cereals with low-fat milk and no sugar.

"Or, I mix natural yogurt, a banana, a teaspoon of raw honey and miller's bran together. It gives me enough food value to last me until lunch time when I eat raw vegetables and nuts.

"The dinner meal is usually a large salad, a bowl of celery or asparagus soup, a glass of natural fruit juice and maybe a piece of cheese. The cheese is optional."

Never introduce a man with a diet like that to your house plants. I know horses and goats who eat better.

My friend explained further about people in other parts of the world whose diets include nothing but natural foods. I remembered the yogurt commercials on television. Eat a lot of yogurt and grow up to be a 112-year-old Russian. Who needs it?

"Don't laugh," he said. "Cultures whose diets are totally natural have no traces of heart disease or cancer or other such diet-related diseases. If Americans would turn to natural foods, it would do wonders for the health of our nation."

That, and eat plenty of liver, I added.

"No liver," he said. "Liver stores all the residues and chemicals the animal takes in from eating his own processed foods. I wouldn't touch liver."

I knew it! Anything that tastes as bad as liver has to be the devil's own doing. Finally, I am absolved. Liver is a lying, indigestible fraud.

Praise the Lord, and pass the roots and berries.

My House and a Word or Two About Cats

I have lived in apartments most of my adult life. I have lived in apartments all over Atlanta. I have lived in two different apartments in Chicago.

My first apartment in Chicago was on the fifth floor of a five-floor building. I had space on the roof and an excellent view of the alley behind the building.

Space on the roof is important in Chicago because that is where you go for cookouts and parties with other residents the two months you wouldn't freeze to death or be blown half way to Gary, Indiana by the wind.

Cookouts and parties on a roof in Chicago are equivalent to cookouts and parties in the backyard in Atlanta. Such occasions are more of an adventure on a roof, however, because you can't get wall-eyed and fall off a backyard.

A good view of the alley is also something nice to have in a Chicago apartment because otherwise you might go days without seeing a single mugging.

My second apartment in Chicago was on the second floor. The people downstairs had cats. Cats are snooty and wouldn't fetch a stick on a bet. They also scratch. I dislike cats.

One night a cat belonging to the people downstairs came into my apartment while I was having dinner. It jumped onto the table and walked in the mashed potatoes. I attempted to drown the cat in the gravy. Never attempt to drown a cat in gravy.

The people downstairs refused to pay for the sticthes.

Several years ago, I lived in an apartment on the south side of Atlanta near the airport. It had one of those fancy, English names like Hampshire on the Lake. Or Oyster on the Half-Shell. I forget which.

Regardless, the noise from airplanes landing and taking off from Hartsfield gave me migraine headaches, and the first time it rained, the apartment flooded.

Pleas to the resident manager's office for help and a pump went unheeded. Finally, I wrote her a letter. "I can no longer live in this carpeted rice paddy," is what I wrote. She finally came over to inspect my apartment and brought her cat. It drowned.

My last apartment was on the northwest side of the city, and the most interesting thing about it was the pool and the girl who sat by it wearing nothing but two strategically placed R.C. caps and a polka-dot loin cloth.

My apartment pool was also where off-duty airline stewardesses came to sunbathe. The girl with the two R.C. caps and the polka-dot loin cloth was *not* an airline stewardess, however.

She was an ex-biology teacher who got fired for adding new dimensions to show-and-tell time.

The purpose for all this background on my apartment living adventures is to tell you I have finally given up apartment living, not to mention another deposit.

I bought a house. One with windows and doors and a leaking faucet in the bathtub. One with trees in the yard and squirrels and birds in the trees. One with gutters to clean and grass to cut. One with taxes and insurance and a high interest rate and dogs who roam in the yard and who had a dinner party in the first batch of garbage I dumped in my very own curbside garbage container.

One my old furniture insults. I have bought automobiles for what a couch and a coffee table costs these days. One with windows to wash and carpets to clean and leaves to rake.

One with bathroom tile that needs *grouting.* Until I bought a house, I thought grouting was something only consenting adults should do and only with the lights off.

But one the sun shines into in the mornings. And one I hoped for and saved for and looked high and low for.

One I wouldn't mind sharing someday.

Maybe I'll buy a cat.

Don't Get Gypped When You Need a Crypt

I started not to write this column. It's about cemetery plots. This is only my third sentence, but I've already got the creeps.

When I was a kid, the old folks used to gather and talk about their cemetery plots. I would leave the room.

When I returned, they had usually progressed to the Fire on Judgment Day. I would leave the room again.

"Where is your plot, Myrtle?" one of the old folks would ask another.

"On the hill."

"Not much shade up there," the dialogue would continue.

"It's peaceful, though. And I overlook the front of the church."

"I'm under the oak tree, next to Maude Bates."

"Won't it be cold in the wintertime?"

"I'm wearing my wool suit."

"The gray one?"

"Gray with black checks."

"You'll be pretty as a picture. If you don't break out."

"Why should I break out?"

"Wool. Maude Bates wore wool, you know. She broke out something awful."

"How do you know that?"

"Her sister Ruby told me. Ruby's on the hill next to me. We're wearing cotton prints."

I can take almost anything else. Dandruff, roaches in the sink, your last proctoscope examination. But not cemetery plots. Cemetery plots are personal, like your underwear size.

And deliver me from advertisements about cemetery plots and their accompanying paraphernalia. Classified ads in the newspaper sell plots like used cars:

"WESTVIEW—4-grave. Terrace B. Shaded, Curbside. Reasonable. Leaving state. Quick sale."

What's so important about being "curbside"? You're going to catch a bus?

Another ad caught my eye the other day:

"DAWN MEMORIAL, (2) plots with vaults, markers and perpetual maintenance. Must sell. Need money!"

That's obvious. Anybody needing money bad enough to hock his own burial vault and marker is one broke hombre.

Television commercials for cemetery plots are even worse. There was the one I borrowed from to begin this column: "We started not to make this commercial," the announcer would open.

And for good reason. It stunk.

". . . But the Deep Six Burial Company wants you to plot now for what the future holds for all of us. Don't be left out in the cold *when that time comes.* You and your loved ones will be eternally grateful you acted now."

I would be eternally grateful if I never saw that commercial again.

Some things simply shouldn't be hard-sold. Cemetery plots head the list. The announcer is somber-slick. The music is sleepy-soft. The plan is "Pay now, die later."

Any day, I expect a commercial for cemetery plots with a singing jingle:

"Pay just two-ninety-five
While you're still alive
So you won't get gypped
When you need a crypt."

I admit I'm easily spooked when it comes to this matter. And I admit I'm in the same mortal boat with everybody else. I will, in fact, need a place to lay me down for the ages.

But I don't want to be reminded of that unsettling fact as I sit in my own living room.

Among other things, it is depressing and causes me to break out like Maude Bates, rest her woolly soul.

I Don't Have Any Children

We were all close once. I thought it had been six, maybe seven years. Somebody else said it had been more like twelve or thirteen.

It was a chance reunion. There was some beer, and we told a few of the old stories again. One was about the time we had Ben E. King at the spring formal at a big, downtown hotel.

A fight broke out. We couldn't remember who started it or who won, but we did recall a lot of glass breaking and being asked never to come back to that particular big, downtown hotel.

They all introduced me to their wives, none of whom seemed particularly interested in hearing a few of the old stories again. Then they pulled out their wallets and showed me pictures of their children.

That's exactly what I needed to see, pictures of their children, but I always make polite remarks at a time like that.

"She's a sweetheart."

"This is when she was an angel in the church play."

"Looks just like you."

"His teacher says he's the brightest kid in her class."

"Fine-looking young man."

"He plays fullback."

They asked if I had any children. Somebody will always ask that, and I will normally answer while staring at the floor.

"No, I don't," I will say. What am I doing? Apologizing? Why do I always feel like I need to offer an explanation?

I don't have any children because I just don't have any. We talked about it. We even tried a couple of times, but nothing ever happened.

And by that time, it was obvious that trying to have a child, under the circumstances, would be . . . stupid. I think that's exactly the word I used. "Stupid."

I have been congratulated often for my farsighted approach to the situation.

"You're better off," people have said to me.

I've also been told I was "lucky."

"You're lucky you never had any children. When you have children, it just makes things a lot worse."

I think it was one of my aunts who said, "At least there weren't any little children to get hurt."

But I like children. Maybe that's a little strong. I don't have anything *against* children, and from what limited knowledge I have of them, there is apparently at least some appeal to their company.

They seem to forgive easily, like dogs, and I am impressed by that.

When they first awaken, they look around for somebody to hold them. I know the feeling.

Thunder frightens children. I'm still not at peaceful terms with thunder, either.

Children give you a fair shot before they decide they don't like you.

They look fresh and cute dressed up, especially when they are dressed up and walking into a church holding their mother's hand.

Children think it's a big deal when you give them a quarter.

I've always wanted to teach a little boy which end of a baseball bat to hold. You would think little boys would be born with that knowledge, but they aren't.

One of the men who was showing me pictures of his children said when you have children you hear the word, "daddy," about a thousand times a day.

That can't be all bad.

Once I took a friend's child on a carnival ride, the Octopus. In the middle of the ride, she said she had to go to the bathroom. I explained the Octopus does not stop when you have to go to the bathroom.

I am positive she did everything in her power to wait until the Octopus ride was over.

The beer gave out about midnight. We promised each other we would get together again soon. Likely, we won't.

You know how it is when you have children.

Airplanes Are Unsafe

I was having a conversation with an airline stewardess. We were not in an airplane, however. I avoid traveling by airplane. Don't get me wrong. I'm not afraid to fly. It is crashing and burning that bothers me. If God had intended man to fly, He would have never given him the rental car and unlimited mileage.

"That's silly," said the stewardess when I told her of my aversion to air travel. "Don't you know that you are safer in an airplane than in an automobile?"

I've heard that bunk before. Anything that goes five miles into the air at 500 miles per hour and they make you strap yourself inside can't be safe.

Automobiles are much safer than airplanes because they don't go as high nor as fast, and they can be pulled over and parked and abandoned, if necessary, at a moment's notice. Try pulling an airplane into the emergency lane when the engine overheats.

I only fly in airplanes in extreme emergencies. Like when the train doesn't go there, the bus company is on strike, or I go temporarily insane.

I even hate airports. First thing you see at an airport is a sign that says "terminal." Airports are noisy, crowded and usually a $15 cab ride from the hotel, plus tip.

The stewardess said she has been flying for twelve years. "I've only been in one real emergency," she said. "I was in a two-engine prop and we lost power in both engines. We were directly over Palm Beach, so we just glided in for a safe landing."

Nothing to it. But engines don't always go out over Palm Beach. Try gliding in to Brasstown Bald, for instance.

I have tried to overcome my difficulties with flying. I decided drinking before boarding would be the answer. I scheduled a flight and then went to the airport bar. A day before the flight.

There isn't enough booze on earth, I discovered, to make me relax on an airplane.

A number of bad things have happened to me on airplanes. Once, I stepped on a woman's violin case while trying to get past her to a window seat. She called me awful names for two hours and tried to hit me with what used to be a violin.

Another time, I had to sit next to a religious nut on an airplane. I had rather be hit on the head with a broken violin than to sit next to a religious nut.

"Brother," he said to me, "do you know the Lord?" I said I knew *of* Him.

"Are you ready to meet Him?" he continued.

I looked out the window. We were 20,000 feet and climbing.

"I thought this was the Milwaukee flight," I said.

I do have some faith in airplane pilots, however. Especially Robert Stack and John Wayne. I know pilots go through rigorous training, and I know they are checked regularly to make sure their hands are still steady on the stick.

When I fly, I like for the pilot to have gray hair and a gorgeous woman awaiting his arrival at our destination. Something to live for, in other words.

"I dated a pilot five years," said the stewardess. "I'll never forget the day we broke up. He called me from the airport, just before takeoff. We had an awful fight and I hung up on him."

"Was he mad?" I asked her.

"Was he mad? He pulled the plane away from the gate and rammed one of the wings into another plane. He always was one to pout."

A pouting pilot. I think I am going to be sick.

My Kind of Town

Chicago isn't really a city. It's a train wreck. Five or six or seven million people live there against their will. Chicago has a river that runs through the middle of town. You can walk across it in the wintertime because it's frozen. You can walk across it in the summertime because it is thick with various forms of waste. Like floating bodies.

Chicago's political system is "vote for the Democrat, or I'll break your arms." It is not safe to ride the city's transit system. Dial "el" for murder.

It is not safe to drive on the city's streets. Every year, hundreds of motorists are lost after driving into potholes which the city repairs once a decade whether they need to or not.

Say something nice about Chicago for a change. OK. There hasn't been a mass murder there in nearly three weeks.

The worst thing about Chicago, of course, is the weather. There is no autumn in Chicago, and there is no spring. Summer lasts an hour and a half. The rest of the time it is winter.

I lived in Chicago two years. It was so cold, my precinct captain

was Frosty the Snowman. A precinct captain is the one who gives
you the bottle of whiskey on election day.

The current winter in Chicago has been the worst since 1912,
the year Mayor Daley was elected. Already this month, there have
been two blizzards. I saw it snow in May once. Welcome to Ice
Station Zero.

There is some humor in all this, however. Something new called
Chicago jokes. A few were offered in a Chicago newspaper the
other day:

How many Chicagoans does it take to drive a car in winter?
Seven. One to steer, six to push.

Why do Chicago-style pizzas have such thick crusts?
What isn't eaten can be used for insulation.

How do you drive a Chicagoan crazy?
Send him or her a $5 gift certificate toward a Florida vacation.

I thought of some Chicago jokes of my own.

How do they start the baseball season in Chicago?
The mayor thaws out the first ball.

*How does a robber disguise himself while holding up a Chicago
liquor store in the wintertime?*
He takes off his ski mask.

Where had your wife rather live than in Chicago?
Wait a minute. Alaska.

I feel sorry for people who still live in Chicago. They should
have their heads examined for brain warts. I especially felt sorry
for them Thursday. Thursday was a spring day in January in
Atlanta.

I even called one of my old Lincoln Avenue haunts—the
Twenty-Three Fifty Pub—to inquire about the health and well-
being of some of my old drinking buddies, the ones who used to
insist Chicago is a nice place to live.

"Your mother's a polar bear," I would say to them just before
the beer-throwing started.

Chuck Dee came to the phone. He runs the joint. I asked about
the weather.

"Colder'n (something I can't print)," he said. "Thirty inches of snow on the ground and more falling."

"Nearly sixty degrees here," I told him.

"That's cold," he said.

"Sixty ABOVE, dummy," I said.

"Go to (somewhere it's at least warm)," he said back.

Chuck lives near the pub.

"The people on my street got together and hired two snowplows to come dig us out," he explained. "The drivers took one look and refused. I'm the only one who can get out. But I had to buy a four-wheel drive jeep to do it."

Some people never learn, which reminds me of another Chicago joke I made up Thursday.

What do you say to a smart Chicagoan?

Welcome South, brother.

• 3 •

COLD BEER AND COUNTRY MUSIC

I fell in love with country music when I was nine years old and somebody slipped a nickel into the juke box at Steve Smith's truck stop in my hometown of Moreland, Georgia, and played a hurtin' song by Hank Williams. Everybody likes beer, of course.

The Best Beer Joint in Georgia

Jim Stone led me inside the "No-Name" beer joint. "This place just ain't been the same," he said, a certain sadness and longing in his voice, "since the monkey died."

The monkey and its passing are another story I will get around to later. Before that, meet the winner of the Lucille's Memorial Best Beer Joint Search Contest, Jim Stone.

Several months ago, I asked for nominations for the best beer joint in the state of Georgia and named it for Lucille, who sold me my first beer. There were contest rules. The juke box had to be all-country, there couldn't be any mixed drinks or cheeseburgers on sale, wives or girlfriends of regulars weren't allowed, neither were smart-aleck college students, and a bottle of imported beer within thirty miles of the place would be grounds for automatic disqualification.

Jim Stone entered the "No-Name" beer joint in Willacoochee. It is called the "No-Name" because it doesn't have a name. A broken Pabst sign outside is the only evidence the one-room building is where a man can break a dry spell. Otherwise:

—— The jukebox is all-country.

—— Beer costs 55 cents. *All* beer, including gloriously cold longnecks.

—— Cans of Vienna sausage adorn the back counter.

—— There is a sign that says, "No Bumming and No Begging." ("They ain't kiddin'," said a regular.)

—— There is another sign that says, "No Gambling: Anybody caught gambling will be 'prosuted.' "

—— There are two pool tables in the back, which is the reason for the gambling sign.

—— There is no air-conditioning. The windows and doors are kept open in the summer, closed in the winter.

—— There is a new paint job on the outside toilet, despite the fact an indoor facility was installed a month ago.

—— You can still use the outdoor toilet if you want to.

—— The regulars inside do a lot of pulpwooding in the swamp, but they are friendly.

—— The bartender's name is "Hoss," and he chews tobacco.

First prize in the Lucille's Memorial Best Beer Joint Search Contest was that I come to the winner's favorite spot and we drink beer and I pick up the tab.

We started as the evening sun was going down on Willacoochee, which straddles the Seaboard Coast Line tracks and Highway 82 between Pearson and Alapaha, on the west end of Atkinson County, a hard day's ride from Atlanta in the flats and piney woods of deep south Georgia.

Jim Stone had driven in from Douglas, where he works for South Georgia College. "A lot of folks come here from Douglas," he explained. "Willacoochee is to Douglas sort of what Hyannis Port is to Boston."

"Hoss" was behind the bar, his jaw bulging. Luther, one of the regulars in overalls, had dropped by. So did Lace Futch, the mayor of Willacoochee, a man of constant good humor. Amos, the jailer, was there and so was Henry, who owns the No-Name.

Henry was proud to know his place had won the contest.

"I can use the business," he said.

"You ain't doing so bad, are you, Henry?" asked Jim Stone.

"I ain't saying for sure," replied Henry, "but I got three head of young'uns at the house, and ain't none of 'em missing no meals."

We sat ourselves down at one of the two tables, the one nearest the jukebox, which Henry turned up because we asked him to. We proceeded with the longnecks.

The hot south Georgia sun poured in through the windows. Tired and thirsty men who sweat for a living poured in through the doors in search of relief for dusty and parched throats. The jukebox blared.

She stood outside the door, not daring to come in. She wore bermudas. She was barefoot in the sand. She held an infant at her hip.

"Your old lady's out there," Henry said to a young man as he pulled on a tall bottle. The young man finished his beer. But slowly. Only then did he walk outside and disappear with his family west on Highway 82.

A slow Seaboard freight passed on the tracks outside. Somebody said Mayor Futch was ready to take on the entire Seaboard Coast Line.

"They got boxcars parked right in the middle of town, and they won't move 'em," the mayor said.

"How long have they been there?" I asked.

"Eight years," he answered.

Jim Stone finally got around to the monkey story. It is fairly complicated.

A few years back, there was a girl in town who was an excellent basketball player. Her family gave her a pet monkey for high school graduation. But the monkey was messy. Her parents told the girl to give the monkey away.

"She brought it here," said Jim Stone. "It was some kind of smart monkey. They trained it to take the change off the table anytime anybody passed out. Everybody's got to earn his keep."

I had to ask how the monkey died.

"Bad diet," Jim Stone explained. "You can't live that long on just beer and peanuts."

"That ain't nothing," interrupted Mayor Futch. "They used to have a coon in here, too. People would come in and the coon would crawl up on their table. They'd fill the ashtrays full of beer and the coon would drink it all."

We were pondering that when the mayor spoke up again.

"I'll tell you something else," he said, "about half drunk, that was one mean coon."

The tab for the entire afternoon was less than $30, and that even included a round of Vienna sausages and Conway Twitty's "We're Not Exactly Strangers" five times on the juke box.

Somebody said it was the only thing the monkey and the coon ever agreed on. It was their favorite song.

Zell and Fuzz

NASHVILLE — The distinguished lieutenant governor of Georgia, Zell Miller, is a big man in Nashville. He knows practically all the country music stars, and they know him.

Zell Miller was instrumental, a lovely choice of words, in helping Don Williams acquire a new drummer for his band from England recently.

For the uninformed, Don Williams was named male vocalist of the year Monday night at the spiffy Country Music Association awards program here.

Zell is also big buddies with Bill Anderson. Ronnie Milsap, who has reached superstar status, was a student of his at Young Harris College. Zell Miller is a country music expert, a country music superfan, and if he is ever elected governor, I would not be surprised if he didn't start work on moving the Grand Ole Opry to Marietta. Make that "May-retta."

Monday afternoon in Nashville, the lieutenant governor went down to old Music Row to The Alamo, Nashville's top shop for rhinestone suits, boots and cowboy hats.

He tried on hats. He priced a $350 pair of boots. But all he bought was a jar of boot polish and a pair of gray socks.

"This is the same way I feel state government should be run," he said, counting out the $3.50 total to the cashier. "You look around at everything you would like to have, but in the end, you buy only the necessities and make do."

A wonderful thing happened to Zell Miller in Nashville this week at the CMA awards show.

Zell met country comedian Jerry Clower, who is from Yazoo City, Mississippi, and who tells funny stories in person and on records for a living. He used to be a fertilizer salesman.

"I've been wanting to meet you, Lieutenant Governor Miller," Jerry Clower said, " 'cause I have done used one of your stories on my latest album, and I give you credit for it. I say, 'This story comes from the lieutenant governor of the great state of Georgia.' "

News that George Busbee had just abdicated the governorship couldn't have made Zell Miller happier.

Later, I asked him to tell me the story. There was a reason for that. He's *our* lieutenant governor, the story happens in Georgia, and we deserve to hear it before the rest of the world.

Ladies and gentlemen, Jerry Clower's budding ghostwriter, Zell Miller:

"This is a true story. It happened up in my hometown of Young Harris. Young Harris is a very small town. We didn't even have a fire department. Not even a volunteer fire department.

"One day, a house caught fire. The whole town gathered around to watch it. We were helpless to put it out. About that time, we saw a pickup truck come over the ridge. It was a local character named Fuzz Chastain. He had his wife with him, all their kids, a cousin or two, and some aunts and uncles.

"Fuzz drove right down to where we were all standing, but he didn't stop. He drove that pickup right into the middle of the fire. He jumped out and so did everybody else. They started beating the fire with anything they could find—even their clothes.

"It took 'em thirty minutes, but danged if they didn't put out the fire. The mayor of Young Harris was there. He said, 'This is the most courageous thing I have ever seen in Young Harris. Let's pass the hat for Fuzz Chastain.'

"They raised $17. The mayor presented the money to Fuzz. 'Fuzz,' he said, 'the people of Young Harris appreciate this heroic act of yours.' Fuzz's hair was singed. His clothes were burned and torn.

" 'But Fuzz, there is one thing I'd like to know,' the mayor went on, 'What are you going to do with this money?'

"Fuzz thought a minute and then said, 'Well, Mr. Mayor, I guess the first thing I ought to do is get the brakes fixed on that pickup.' "

If Zell Miller's new "career" takes off, don't worry if he can mix show business with politics. Lest we forget, in many respects, they're the same.

Dreaming at the Twilite

It was Ladies Night at the Twilite Club down on Stewart Avenue, but it was too cold for a crowd. Nights like this are for covering up early, even if the bedroom is a lonely place. There is always the cat.

The band was allegedly country. Mostly, it was loud and did too many Elvis numbers. The singer's shirt was unbuttoned nearly all the way down. That's not country.

"Y'all got any requests?" he asked the sparse audience.

"Yeah," said an old girl sitting at the table next to mine. She was drinking salty dogs. "Turn that thang down."

Big Jim Cook had an easy night. He's the bouncer. The Twilite Club isn't a rough place, by any means, but like the lady who runs it said, "We're getting a little more riff-raff since the Nugget Club burned down."

Jim Cook is twenty-seven and big as a Haggard hit single. He's 6-4 and 240 and he still goes home to Milner, which is near Griffin, on the weekends to see his mother. "I ain't nothing," he says, "but an old country boy from the woods."

He probably could have been more than that, and may yet be. That is his story. Jim Cook was a good enough high school basketball player that Georgia Tech offered a scholarship. He turned it down. "I just didn't know what I wanted to do," is his explanation.

That's not the best reason in the world to pass up a free college education, but like the man said, ten years later it will have to do.

The band *was* loud, but we talked between ear-splitting choruses, and I found out what Jim Cook wants to be more than anything else is a famous professional wrestler. Granny says *rassler*.

He used to be skinny, he said, but he wandered into one of those health spas one day and now he could walk around with a Datsun on his back.

"Some of the wrestlers come in here," he said. "They got me interested. You can make a lot of money."

You can. You can also get thrown on the floor and crab-locked and full-Nelsoned until you are a walking bruise. And you can spend a great deal of your time jumping around in your underwear in front of screaming crowds packed into tank town high school gymnasiums. Wrestling has its bush leagues, too. Verne Gagne and Lou Thetz stayed at the Ritz and drank call brands. Jim Cook is doing Carrollton and Porterdale.

He was married, but that ended in divorce and one child. He was a yardman at an auto transport company in Atlanta. That ended when he was laid off. A wrestler now retired, one Rocket Monroe, helped him learn the basics, and Jim Cook took off for California and Canada to seek his wrestling fortune.

He didn't find it. Vancouver can be rotten lonely and rainy. He worked his way back South, back through Kansas City and Oklahoma. A man in Oklahoma told him to go home and find somebody to teach him to wrestle.

"That's the problem," the big man said. "Most of the guys I know have to wrestle every night. They don't have the time to train me."

He insists wrestling isn't fake. "You can get hurt if you don't know what you're doing," he said. No matter where he wrestles, the place is packed. Watching wrestling is like eating collards. If you're hooked, you're hooked.

He's gone against some of the biggies in the area: The Anderson Brothers, Stan Hansen, Dick Slater, a Korean guy whose name he

can't spell, Bill White, and a masked fellow who calls himself The
Executioner. Mostly, he loses. "But I'm a good guy," he explained.
"The people always cheer me on."

Jim Cook stayed around until the Twilite Club went dark for a
few restful hours. "The only time we really have trouble," he had
said, "is when somebody comes in from another part of town and
doesn't know what kind of place this is. Usually, by the time anybody is ready to do more than talk, he's too drunk to fight."

When he finally went home, it was to a room at the Alamo Plaza
Motel, a southside relic. There would hopefully be the chance to
work out the following day. And maybe there will also be the
chance someday to get off the bottom of the cards, to get out of the
preliminaries and into the main events. To make a name. To make
a buck. To be there in the City Auditorium on Friday nights when
the masses come and the lights are shining brightly.

A country boy from Milner has a dream.

The Den Mother of Country Music

NASHVILLE — They put Tootsie Bess to rest on a snowy hillside
in Nashville Tuesday afternoon. When she died of cancer at sixty-
four the other day, they should have lowered every flag in the city
to half-mast. She was somebody. She was the den mother of country music.

Without her, there might not have been the stardom and the
music of people like Tom T. Hall. Or Kris Kristofferson. Or Roger
Miller. Or Johnny Rodrigues. Or Hank Williams, or any number
of pickers and singers who have made what otherwise would have
been nothing more than Chattanooga North into a multi-million
dollar recording Mecca called Music City U.S.A.

Without her, many who stayed and finally caught their dreams
might have long since caught the next bus back home. Like a man
said at Tootsie's funeral Tuesday, "You can find rhinestones and

applause in Nashville, but before you do, it can be the loneliest place in the world."

Hattie Louise "Tootsie" Bess ran a beer joint in Nashville at Fifth and Broadway called Tootsie's Orchid Lounge. There was a back door. It led to an alley that led to the stage entrance of the old Ryman Auditorium, for years the home of the Grand Ole Opry.

Grant Turner, the Opry announcer, said, "You could leave Tootsie's at 7:58 and still be on stage at the Opry at 8 o'clock." So many did just that.

When Tom T. Hall first came to Nashville, he nearly starved. Tootsie fed him. Tootsie encouraged him. Tootsie gave him pocket money. Today, Tom T. Hall sells millions of records and trucks on television.

Kris Kristofferson worked construction and swept floors in Nashville while trying to peddle his music. He was one of Tootsie's pets. She kept him going until another star was born.

Roger Miller was a Nashville bellhop. He would write one of his biggest hits, "Dang Me," in a booth at Tootsie's.

"She ran a beer joint," said Tom T. Hall, "but to young songwriters and musicians, she was a small finance company, a booking agent, and a counsellor."

Maybe Ernest Tubb put it even better: "Tootsie," he said, "was the softest touch in town."

I was in her place only once. But I remember the beer being cold and the atmosphere being warm and Tootsie saying as my party left, "Y'all come back when you can stay longer."

Her juke box had million sellers. It also had non-sellers. When nobody else would play a youngster's record, Tootsie would put it next to "Hello Walls," and give the kid the best chance she could.

She kept order with a hatpin. Get rowdy and out you went at the point of her hatpin. Come back tomorrow and apologize, and all was forgiven.

There were five inches of fresh snow on the ground in Nashville Tuesday. Still, the funeral home was packed with people and flowers.

The registry was a country music who's who. Mel Tillis sent

flowers. There was a wreath from Ben Smathers and his mountain cloggers. Ernest Tubb and his son Justin sent a heart-shaped arrangement. There was a break in the middle of the heart. It was pierced with a hatpin.

Roy Acuff sat down front for the services. One of the Wilburn Brothers was close to him. Included in the grieving family was Tootsie's son-in-law, who is an Opry drummer. Tom T. Hall was one of the pallbearers. Grant Turner got up and said a few words. And Connie Smith stood behind Tootsie's lavender casket and sang "In the Sweet By and By," "Amazing Grace," and "How Great Thou Art." She has never sounded better.

Tootsie had friends who weren't stars. "She was just as happy to see a ditch digger walk in as the biggest name in town," said a friend. Sitting next to a millionaire singer at the funeral was a man in a service station outfit. He hadn't had time to wash the grease off his hands.

The preacher read a telegram from Tennessee Sen. Howard Baker. He talked about the necessity of loving one another and said Mrs. Bess, as he called her, performed that task exactly as the Good Book intended.

It could be the Good Lord likes the company of a bighearted saloonkeeper, too.

Willie at the White House

WASHINGTON — People wearing bags over their heads and carrying signs that screamed about "massacres" in their native Iran paraded in front of the White House Wednesday evening.

To the north of the city at Camp David, three powerful leaders of three powerful nations struggled to find a way to bring peace to another troubled land.

The papers were filled with stories of death and destruction in Nicaragua, and half the world is on strike.

But the night was clear, and cool and the moon was full and bright in Washington Wednesday. And out on the south lawn of the White House, a million miles from everything else, a bearded man wearing a red bandana took a long pull from a wine bottle and commenced to sing.

He sang "Whiskey River" first; then he sang "Crazy" and "Amazing Grace" and "Georgia" and something called "Blue Eyes Crying in the Rain." As he sang "Blue Eyes Crying in the Rain" I had a thought, probably an outrageous one, but at least worth a moment of consideration:

Jimmy Carter didn't make his own party Wednesday night, the one he threw to honor stockcar drivers. His wife announced to the crowd that "only something the magnitude of the summit talks would have kept him away."

He made a mistake by not coming. And he made a mistake by not bringing Egypt's Sadat and Israel's Begin with him.

Sit the two of them down together in front of Willie Nelson, I thought. Bring the people with the bags over their heads inside, too. Give them all a cold beer and let them listen to Willie Nelson. After "Blue Eyes Crying in the Rain," who would still want to fight?

Wednesday night was Jimmy Carter fulfilling a promise. When he was governor of Georgia, he made it an annual practice to host stockcar drivers and even sportswriters at the mansion on West Paces Ferry.

You know about stockcar racing. Stockcar racing isn't Watkins Glen or spiffy gentlemen in sleek Porsches and Ferraris. It is Talledega and Daytona and Atlanta International Raceway and beer and fried chicken and a punch in the nose because you said a Chevrolet can whip a Dodge or, worse, you insulted the glorious memory of Fireball Roberts.

"Jimmy told us if he ever got to be president," explained driver David Pearson, "we would share in some of the glory. Here we are."

And there they were. Pearson, Petty, Waldrip, Yarborough, and Bill France, the head kabolla of stockcar racing. And even some sportswriters and even Billy Carter, and especially Willie Nelson, who sang with Amy and Rosalynn and Billy's wife, Sybil.

The night was heavy with doubleknit and denim.

The Washington papers the next day didn't quite know what to make of the affair. They said it did prove we are under the reign of a populist president. They went into great detail concerning the Carters' love for stockcar racing and explained stockcar racing grew in the South from an earlier preoccupation with running moonshine.

"I ain't never run moonshine," Richard Petty told a reporter. "but I don't know about the rest of my family."

I go back to those parties at the governor's mansion. The first one was a flop because Rosalynn had charge of the food and entertainment. She offered an exotic menu that included fish-like things that still had their eyes. The entertainment was an operatic trio.

I can still see A. J. Foyt shifting uncomfortably from one cowboy boot to another and Jabe Thomas driving to the front of the mansion in his mechanic's truck. I can still hear somebody saying, "This would make Curtis Turner roll over in his grave." Rosalynn Carter stepped onto the bandshell behind the White House Wednesday night and apologized for all that. She had learned her lesson. The fare this evening was beer and wine and roast beef and ham and corn bread. The program announced. "Selections by Willie Nelson."

I could probably dabble around in all this for some hidden political meaning. But the heck with that.

What happened Wednesday night at the home of the president of the United States was a large group of mostly Southern people got together in the backyard for a picnic and to listen to one of their own sing his red bandana off. Andy Jackson used to give the same kind of parties here, and he wound up on the $20 bill.

In the middle of that singing, when people had squared off to clog on the lawn, a fellow I know from Georgia came to my table and whispered in my ear:

"My great-grandfather was wounded at the Battle of Sharpsburg. He was captured at Gettysburg, He had to limp all the way home to Georgia. If he could see this tonight, he'd think we won after all.''

Sweet Innocence

That was her daddy, the girl said, playing with the country band that performed, sort of, in one corner of the room. They played the old songs—hungry songs and cheatin' songs—and they made them sound even older.

Her mama was in and out, too. She was a stout, tightfaced woman and she gave the appearance of running things. A would-be rowdy was rendered nearly peepless after mama suggested his conduct was reaching the bouncing stage.

It doesn't matter the name of the town or the name of the joint, because there are maybe a million towns and million joints just like them.

Picture a two-lane highway running through what seems like nowhere on a warm Georgia spring night. Suddenly, up ahead, the glare of neon is blinking and beckoning. Park some trucks around. Behold, the local fast crowd in its natural habitat.

The girl worked feverishly behind the bar while daddy played and mama patrolled. She was pretty. Dark hair and dark eyes. Plump, a little, but pleasingly so. She wore pink chiffon. Tight pants and a blouse that exposed little, but enough to gather the eyes of the gentleman customers seated around on the bar stools.

I judged her innocent somehow, and trained to perform. At her obviously tender age, could she know what her audience was thinking as she moved gracefully back and forth behind the bar? Likely not.

They ordered beer, of course, and from some unseen cache she produced it in cold, longneck bottles. They were emptied nearly as fast as she could bring more.

There was booze, too. That was surprising, this far into the hinterlands. I wondered to a man next to me how long the county had had liquor.

"Long as there's been anybody around to drink it, I guess," he said. Then, he corrected himself. "You mean how long's it been legal? Four or five years, I guess."

And the Baptists and the bootleggers are still fighting it, somebody added.

I watched the girl. She had been trained well. Her performance was splendid. I waited for a slip, something that would unveil that innocence that seemed unfit for midnight in a smoky, backroads saloon. It never came.

A youngster sat alone at the end of the bar, nursing a beer.

"One more?" the girl asked.

The youngster nearly blushed from her attention. He held the bottle against a light. It was nearly empty.

"Believe I've had enough," he said.

"Just one more?" the girl persisted. "For me?"

"One more," the youngster said. He seemed pleased he had pleased her.

She even sang. Daddy played while she sang. The place was hers all over again.

"Sounds just like Linda Ronstadt, don't she?" the man with the liquor information said to me.

I agreed. It's smart, I figured, for a stranger to agree.

The band took a break, and the girl asked nobody in particular for money to play the jukebox. To a man, her subjects reached into their pockets for change.

The chosen one marched to the jukebox and obediently pushed the buttons as the girl called out the numbers of her favorite songs.

The crowd began to thin later. There were no more calls for drinks. The girl walked to where I was sitting and propped herself on the bar. She asked where I was from. I told her.

"I was in Atlanta once," she said. She named the hotel. "I didn't like it. That place is too big for me."

There is was. Simple girl, simple tastes. Maybe one day she can leave this, I thought. Find some nice fellow with a good job and raise a family.

"Daddy gone?" the girl asked a waitress, who nodded yes.

"Mama, too?" she asked next. Mama was gone, too.

"Damn, it's about time," said the girl, reaching for a bottle of vodka on the shelf. She filled a glass and heaved down its contents in one hard gulp.

• 4 •

THOSE WERE
THE DAYS

The first column in this section is about my fifteenth year high school reunion that turned out to be a tremendous success. One of my ex-wives came. She looked terrific. Dudley Stamps, who was a good friend in school, also came to the reunion.

He said to me, "I see your damn picture in the newspaper sometimes, but I don't read any of that garbage." When we had some beer later, I hugged his neck anyway.

The last column in this section is about Bill Johnson, who was a classmate in college. He died. I wish I could hug his neck one more time.

The Class of '64

The fellow who was president of my high school senior class called the other day to ask a favor. He wants me to write something witty and clever to be used as an invitation to our fifteenth year class reunion next summer.

We never had a tenth year reunion, which was just as well with me. The principal's office statute of limitations probably doesn't run out in ten years. They might still have had something on me.

Like there was the book I never got around to returning to the school library. The posse didn't come back until the early seventies. Our librarian was also the principal's wife, and she ran the library with an iron hand. Nuclear power plants are maintained with less regimentation.

I was remembering some of the library rules at my high school:

——Thou shalt not touch a book unless your hands have been scrubbed clean and thoroughly inspected by the head librarian. ("A smudge on a book is an insult to literature.")

——Thou shalt not wear wristwatches or bracelets into the library because a wristwatch or a bracelet could make a scratch on one of the library tables, God forbid.

(I am convinced anybody caught scratching a library table at my high school would have been dragged out behind the auditorium and shot, not to mention having his or her library privileges taken away.)

——Thou shalt not talk while in the library, nor giggle nor grunt nor pull a chair from under a table so as to make the noise a chair being pulled from under a table will inevitably make.

(Once a fat girl, who was stronger than I, punched me in the belly in the library because I wouldn't give her the sports section of the newspaper. I grunted from the punch and attempted to flee for fear of further blows.

(In my haste, I pulled my chair from under the table and it made a noise. I had to stay after school every day for a week and my stomach hurt for a month. The fat girl's nickname was "Mean Mama," incidentally.)

Irregardless—which isn't a word but was used a hundred times a day by one of the coaches—I still look back on my high school years with favor.

I was on the baseball team and the basketball team, and I was in the Key Club and I had a steady girlfriend, which is another reason I wasn't particularly disturbed when we had no tenth year reunion.

The last time I saw my steady girlfriend, who later became much more than that, she was loading our living room furniture, my stereo, the bed, and the washer and dryer into the back of a truck.

Who knows what she might still have been in the market for?

Frankly, I am puzzled as to what to write witty and clever for the invitation.

I can say we'll all drink a few beers, likely, and we won't have to hide behind Robert's and Alf's drive-in to do it.

We'll take a look at one another and say things like, "You haven't changed a bit" when what we really mean is, "I wouldn't have known you in a million years because the last time I saw you, you had hair."

We'll see who is fat now who didn't used to be, and who lost weight and who is still obnoxious and who got rich and who wouldn't kiss you goodnight for love nor money in school but has been pregnant practically every day since graduation. And who has retained all his hair and his slim, boyish figure. Like me.

We'll listen to the old songs and tell a lie or two.

And maybe for old times' sake, I'll even have a dance with my steady girlfriend who later became much more than that while somebody sings, "In the Still of the Night."

Come to think of it, fifteen years later is a perfect time to have a high school reunion. It's a short enough period for the good memories to be fresh and for the ravages of age to have taken only a soft toll.

And long enough to have forgiven an overdue library book, a punch in the belly, and even the night I walked into an empty house and found out for the first time adulthood isn't all it was cracked up to be.

They Were Playing Our Songs

The three of us were children of the forties, but we had left the campus when the trouble began. We were born of men back from the war and the women who waited for them to come home.

We barely remember Korea. My daddy was gone two years, and I really never knew why. The name Harry Truman rings a vague bell. The thing I remember most about Ike was how the people down home cursed him for spending too much time playing golf at Augusta.

Kennedy was ours, but we lost him in high school. Vietnam was festering during our college days, but on a sleepy Deep South campus, it would take longer for the explosion of dissent to finally come.

After school, one of us—ordered to do so—went to the fight. The other two, lucky as hell, stayed home and learned about making a living.

We made the same fraternal pledge fifteen years ago. That tie still binds us somehow. One of us is losing his hair. Another has

put on a few pounds. I get down in my back occasionally and I
don't sleep as well as I used to.

Monday night was a reunion of sorts. It is rare we can be together as a threesome for an evening out anymore.

But this was special. They were playing our songs at a club
called the Harlequin. We wouldn't have missed it.

First, you must get this picture: The year is 1964. The band is
black and loud. Beer cans are illegal on campus. There was such a
thing in those days, however, as "Humdinger" milkshake cups.
They would hold two full cans until they became soggy and fell
apart. A date must be selected carefully. She must not mind beer
on her skirt. There were a lot of good women like that in 1964.

And the band would play until midnight, time to beat the cur-
few back to the girls' dorms. The frolic before was always grand
and glorious because, as that campus anthem went, we came to
college not for knowledge, but to raise hell while we're here.

Our music was a soulful strut. Maurice Williams and the Zodi-
acs, "Stay;" The Isley Brothers, "Twist and Shout;" The Tempta-
tions, "My Girl;" The Drifters, "Save the Last Dance for Me;"
Marvin Gaye and the classic, "Stubborn Kind of Fellow."

And two more groups, hallowed be their names: The Atlanta
Tams. The Showmen.

We were on the edge of our seats Monday night. And then,
there they were. Four black men from Norfolk, Virginia. Four
black men who can dance and sing and take you back where, the
Lord knows, you never wanted to leave in the first place.

Four black men called The Showmen who put "39-21-46" on a
record years ago.

"We're gonna take the roof off this place," they said, and they
did.

The Tams were next. "Atlanta's own Atlanta Tams," announced the announcer. They have aged, the Tams. But their
voices still blend in perfect, deep harmony, and when they sang
"What Kind of Fool?" everybody in the house was nineteen years
old again.

As is the custom, we went down front to the stage before the night was over. We sang and we danced along. Our parents did the same to Big Band swing. A group of teenyboppers went crazy over a child named Shaun Cassidy at the Omni the other night. Who knows what sound will attract our children?

But does it really matter? Music, any kind of music, is memories and sometimes hope for the future. Music can soothe, music can hurt. Music can be lost loves and old friends. Music can give advice worth heeding.

"Listen to that," said one of us to the other two Monday night. "They're right, you know."

The Tams were singing. It was one of their old songs. You have missed something if you have never heard it. Three fellows bound for middle-age gathered in every word:

"Be Young.

"Be Foolish.

"Be Happy."

When the Smoke Had Cleared

Dorsey Hill still laughs about the night I came through fraternity rush at the Sigma Pi house in Athens.

"Damn'dest sight I ever saw," he says. "You were wearing white socks and black, pointed-toe shoes, and your head was skinned. I mean *skinned.* I said, 'Where on earth did THAT come from?' "

But they took in the skinhead anyway at the house on Milledge Avenue, the one with the white columns, and there were some high times the next four years.

I forget exactly who went to put the Chi Omega owl to the torch. The Chi Omega sorority house was across the street from ours, and they were an uppity bunch. One year they built a paper owl, a huge thing, for rush.

We were sitting on our front porch in those marvelous rocking chairs, and somebody thought it would be a good idea to burn the owl.

Every firetruck in Athens showed up to put it out. So did Dean Tate, dean of University of Georgia men. When the smoke had cleared, we were on something called "social probation."

That meant we couldn't have another party until every member had graduated from school, had fulfilled his military obligation, and had fathered at least two legitimate children.

In retrospect, it was worth it. Fifty silly sorority girls, outraged and bewildered, watching their precious paper owl go up in a glorious blaze. Strike another one for dear old Sigma Pi.

I could do this all day. There was the basement we called the "Boom-Boom Room." Beware, young coed, to enter there. It was in the "Boom-Boom Room" where we administered a water-drinking torture called "Cardinal Puff" during initiation. A pledge almost died after "Cardinal Puff" one night.

Maybe that is what started it. Sigma Pi once thrived. We had the captain of the football team, the captain of the basketball team. But hard times came along.

I heard they had to sell that beautiful old house to pay their way out of debt. I heard the membership had fallen off to almost nothing. I heard the university had even taken away the charter and that Sigma Pi had died a quiet, slow death on the campus.

I shed a quick tear, but nothing more. It's been a long time.

But there was a telephone call last week. It was from a Georgia coed. She had a sense of urgency in her voice.

"You've got to help," she said.

"Help who?" I answered.

"Sigma Pi at Georgia," she went on. "I'm dating this guy who's a member. They're trying to make a comeback, but they're about to go bankrupt. They lost a couple of pledges who were supposed to move into the house. They needed their money for rent. One of them joined the Navy."

I called the Sigma Pi house in Athens. The president answered the telephone. We used to have eighty members. "We've got eleven," he said. We sent more than that to burn the Chi Omega owl.

The new house is being rented from a university faculty member, the young man said. The current members are trying to hold on to the house until more members can be pledged. More members, more money.

"We even keep the heat turned off," he said, "to save money."

There are no parties, the president told me, because there is no money for parties. There are no meals at the house because who can afford cooks? What Sigma Pi in Athens needs and wants is some help from the alumni. A donation, maybe, at least a visit to help with rush.

"Just some encouragement," said the president.

That's not much to ask. I'll try to get up a group and come over, I said. We'll have a few cold ones and talk about it. And afterwards maybe we'll all go over to Chi Omega and apologize.

In a pig's eye, we will.

Sweetheart of Sigma Chi

How I got invited to a University of Georgia fraternity party at my age isn't the story here. The story is what I saw when I went there.

It was the Sigma Chi's annual gathering to select a chapter sweetheart. Sigma Chis the nation over take selecting a chapter sweetheart seriously because somebody once immortalized young ladies so chosen with a popular song entitled, appropriately enough, "Sweetheart of Sigma Chi."

A banquet preceded the party. I don't know what I expected. I had seen *Animal House*. I knew that it was only a short time ago the college campus was a social battleground. Sometimes, it was just a battleground.

But what, I asked myself, are the prevailing moods and customs of the campus on this, the eve of the 1980s?

I knew about the early sixties. It was button-down, slick-it-back, eat, drink and chase Mary in the tight skirt and monogrammed sweater. The late sixties and early seventies were angry and hip and taking things that made you crazy and wearing clothes to look the part.

The Sigma Chis on this night came dressed as a *GQ* ad. They were three-pieced and button-downed and blown-dried almost to a man. Their dates were clones from the Phi Mu house fifteen years ago.

The chapter president, whose hair was shorter than mine, opened with a moving invocation. Gentlemen rose from their seats when ladies excused themselves from the tables. The dinner lasted well over an hour. Nobody threw a single morsel of food.

When the new sweetheart was introduced, the chapter stood as one and sang her their delicate, obviously inspired rendition of the sweetheart song while she cried. Donna Reed would have played her part. John Belushi would have been asked to leave.

There was some loosening up when the party began, but the frolic that followed wouldn't have qualified as even a mild public disturbance.

The band played Marvin Gaye's "Stubborn Kind of Fellow," "Sixty Minute Man," and the Temptation's "My Girl." I know all the words to all three songs. A young man asked for something by Jackie Wilson, and the band gave him "Lonely Teardrops." Who turned back the time machine?

The booze was mostly beer. Somebody had a half-gallon of Jim Beam bourbon and was pouring it into Coca-Cola. The smokers I saw were pulling on Marlboros.

Later in the evening, a small ice fight broke out—it always did—and everybody danced the "Gator." I know grown people who still dance the "Gator," which involves lying on the floor and acting like a half-crazed reptile with a bad case of the shakes.

The University of Georgia was never a leader in the radical league and the war is over now and things are quieter everywhere, but it did occur to me after the Sigma Chi party that perhaps life on the campus has returned to normal, sis-boom-bah.

—— Fraternities and sororities, spurned by many students just a few years ago, are making a big comeback at Georgia. "We are nearly overrun during rush," a Sigma Chi told me.

—— Pot smoking is still prevalent among some students, I was told, but "drinking is back stronger than ever." Sigma Chi fines members caught smoking pot in the fraternity house.

—— Political activism is down on the Georgia campus. SDS is dead and gone. The student body president ran with a bag over his head, the "Unknown Candidate" with no platform. He won in a walk.

The strongest and most active group on campus, believe it or not, is the Young Americans for Freedom, a conservative, pro-Reagan outfit.

"They don't want to stop a war," said an editor at the student newspaper, "they want to start one."

Wonders never cease, and spring quarter approaches. Let's go get a six-pack and have a panty raid.

One for Bill Johnson

ATHENS — Winter quarter was a sinus headache that seemed to linger on and on. The glory of the fall and football had passed. Springtime on the University of Georgia campus was always brightness and color and cold beer in tall cups and young things from Fitzgerald and Dalton whose mommas would have fainted had they known their babies were parading around in public dressed like that. And would it all ever return again and save us from January's gloom?

There was only a trickle of people about the campus Monday. Joggers ran up Lumpkin Street. Will this generation's legacy be a pair of worn running shoes and a green sweatsuit? The Campus Crusade for Christ is presenting *Master of Illusion* this week. One of the sorority houses has a banner hanging outside congratulating a sister for being accepted to the Harvard Law School. Girls used to go to college to find a husband.

But things change. There is even a sign now at the entrance to the athletic department training room in the Georgia Coliseum that reads, "Women are in the training room. Remember to wear

your shorts." I was thinking of some names like Rissmiller and
Swinford and Ridlehuber as I read that sign. Would they have
stood for such encroachment? Women in the training room, in-
deed.

Who can come back here—even in the depths of the winter dol-
drums—and not launch himself into a sentimental journey. Boys
become men here. Gangly, chirping girls become sophisticated
women. How many of us had that first, heady taste of sin on these
grounds? I recall being anxious to leave. I was out of my mind.

Bill Johnson loved Georgia. He loved everything about it. We
were in the same, overloaded boat. We both had school, and we
both—by choice—had work as well. Bill Johnson was employed by
an Athens radio station. I worked for an Athens newspaper.

How do friendships begin? He was "the voice" of Athens High
School sports. I was second on a two-man sports department totem
pole. The boss covered the Bulldogs. I had Athens High. My
friend Bill Johnson and I were together in a thousand rickety,
crowded press boxes in places like Gainesville and Augusta and
Hartwell and Elberton.

He was good at what he did. Bill Johnson was barely past
twenty, but there could be no question as to his promise as a sportscaster. His voice was smooth, yet strong. There were those nights
after games we would drive back to Athens together and fantasize
about our futures.

"Do you think," he would ask, "we'll ever get to the big time?"

I reckoned that we would. We promised if one of us made it and
the other did not, the friendship would last. I have never made a
more sincere promise.

There is something about those days of dreaming. There are no
limits in an ambitious mind. Bill Johnson would be as good and as
important as Ed Thilenius someday. And I would be paid to write a
story about a ball game for an Atlanta newspaper.

The last time I saw Bill Johnson was the day he graduated from
Georgia. We had a few last beers together and said how much we
would miss each other. He also had to leave a young wife in Ath-

ens for a short military obligation. But then he would be back and look out, Lindsey Nelson.

That was March 1966. Spring quarter was beautiful that year. We wrote back and forth. He was stationed somewhere in Texas.

Came the autumn and a wonderful Georgia football team. You remember. Kirby Moore. Kent Lawrence. George Patton. Bill Stanfill.

There was the second half comeback at Auburn that gave Vince Dooley his first Southeastern Conference title. Undefeated Georgia Tech fell the next week in Sanford Stadium. And Georgia would go on to the Cotton Bowl and belittle Southern Methodist.

Somewhere tucked away I have Bill Johnson's last letter. He was ill, he said. It was the first I knew about it. Some crazy blood infection. But he said don't worry. He said the doctors were thinking of letting him go to Dallas to see Georgia in the Cotton Bowl.

A week later, on December 7, Bill Johnson died. He was twenty-three.

The church up in Summerville, his hometown, was packed. When we carried him through town to the cemetery, the old men stopped on the streets and covered their hearts with their hats. The young widow cried hard.

Monday, as I walked across the campus, I remembered another promise. I told Bill Johnson I would mention him one day in a column if I ever got a job with a big city newspaper.

This is that mention. It's for a friend, a long time gone.

THE VIEW FROM LEFT FIELD

I knew it was time for me to get out of sportswriting when I covered the 1978 Super Bowl game between Dallas and Denver and enjoyed the halftime show that featured dogs catching frisbees more than I did the football game.

I will still fall into a sports column now and then, however. It's comfortable there, like an old pair of sneakers.

At the Ball Game With My Dad

I would have taken my father out to the ball game Tuesday night. I would have taken him to the Atlanta Stadium to see Pete Rose try to break Wee Willie Keeler's hitting streak record.

His birthday is Saturday. He would have been sixty-six. A trip to the ball game would have been a nice present from a son to his father.

He was an athlete himself, my dad. And he was a strapping man with alleged blinding speed in his youth. He was taller than Pete Rose, but similar in stocky frame. One time he picked up the back of a 1949 Hudson. I saw him do it.

My father would have loved Tuesday night at the ball park. Nice summer evening. Big, noisy crowd. My father always enjoyed singing the national anthem at baseball games.

He had a big voice, a booming voice that could cut you down at one hundred yards when it broke into "He Leadeth Me" or our national anthem, his two favorite songs. He always sang along when they played the national anthem, no matter where or what event. One time I said to him, "I wish you wouldn't sing so loud. It's embarrassing."

He said to me, "Son, it's embarrassing when you don't sing along with me."

Tuesday night, just before Pete Rose stepped up to bat, going

71

for forty-five straight, my father and I would have stood shoulder-to-shoulder and sung the national anthem together.

Pete Rose is my father's kind of man, I was thinking when Rose approached the plate in the first inning. Just before the game began, he had his picture made with a crippled boy and put his hat on the crippled boy's head.

"Look at the way that man moves," my father would have said of Rose. "He doesn't waste a motion. He has speed. He has strength. He has determination. That's the kind of man you want in a foxhole with you."

My father was a soldier. A damn good one.

His only objection to Pete Rose might have been Rose's hair. I noticed it precariously near his shoulders. His ears disappeared weeks ago. My father wore a crew cut. He thought everybody else should.

"I'll never get used to long hair on a ballplayer or a soldier," he might have said as Larry McWilliams of the Braves threw the first pitch of the ball game—a curve—"It's not what the Lord intended."

The curve to Rose is low for ball one. And then a foul deep to right that misses being a double by five feet. A fast ball outside, a curve catches the inside corner, the count goes full, two more fouls, then ball four. The streak holds at forty-four.

I never saw a major league baseball game with my father. We saw plenty of service ball together. He once coached the Fort Benning team. Coached in a Hawaiian shirt and a straw hat.

Later, we bummed around South Georgia one summer. My father had fallen on hard times, but he kept a ten-year-old fed and cared for during three of the best months of my life.

That summer, we spent night after hot South Georgia night fighting gnats and eating peanuts in broken-down Class D parks in Waycross and Moultrie and Tifton where something called the Georgia-Florida League still had life.

There is something special about a man with his son at a baseball game. A man and his son sat next to me Monday night when Pete Rose extended his batting streak to forty-four. As Pete strode

to the plate for the first time, the boy asked his dad if he would take
him to the rest room.

"Not now, son," said the father. "Not now. Pete Rose is batting."

The boy held on, uncomfortably, but appearing to understand
the necessity of the effort.

When a man takes his son to a baseball game, I think, it estab-
lishes a link, one that won't easily be broken even in the face of a
subsequent premature parting that might leave other scars.

I know that to be a fact.

Rose came up for a second time. "Let's go, Pete," my father
would have screamed, loud enough to be heard in LaGrange.
What the heck. Let him have his fun.

First pitch, Rose swings. A shot up the middle. Young McWilliams' gloved hand appears from nowhere and spears the drive.
Rose drops his bat and gives the youngster a hand. Mostly, my
father would have enjoyed the game Tuesday night because it was
a vivid American scene. It was an act of patriotism, somehow, to
have been there.

He would have looked at his fellow Americans eating hot dogs
and drinking beer, he would have heard their cheers for the home
runs by Horner and Murphy, and he would have said something
like, "This is why your daddy went to war, son. This is what we
fought to keep."

Rose is up again. The inning is the fifth. The game is tied, 3-3. A
fake bunt, ball one. Another ball. Then a ground out to short. The
tension builds.

Now, it is the seventh. The brutal Gene Garber is pitching for
the Braves. A runner is on. One out. A fast ball strike on the
outside corner. Two straight balls. A foul tip, the count is even.
Then, another shot by Rose, toward left, the opposite field. But
Horner is there for the out and a double play.

A final chance, and only that, remains. The ninth. The game has
turned to slaughter. The Reds, for once, are the victims, 16-4. Atlanta has twenty-one hits. Even Garber has one. Pete Rose, whose
name even sounds like a line drive, has none.

Two outs. Rose at the bat. "Pete! Pete! Pete!" the stadium is begging.

The first pitch from Garber. An attempted drag bunt to third goes foul. Two straight balls. A foul tip.

The ball leaves Garber's hand. A split second later, we will know.

Strike three. Swinging. It is over.

What Pete Rose did—hit safely in forty-four straight games—wasn't a man on the moon, I reminded myself as the stadium lights dimmed. It wasn't a lonely flight across the Atlantic or the first heart transplant.

But it was a good and honorable thing, a fierce man with a bat in his hand, playing a boy's game as it was meant to be played.

And I am thankful I had the chance to witness part of it, even the bitter end.

Tuesday night at the ball game, me and my dad had a helluva good time.

A Case of the Bleeps

I missed Pete Rose's post-game television interview Tuesday night after he had failed to extend his batting streak.

I was busy typing in the press box. I never promised the news editor a Rose column, but it seemed the thing to do what with the excietment the hitting streak had generated.

I understand it was an interesting interview. Ted Turner's nationwide network carried it, and little old ladies coast-to-coast were swallowing their snuff.

Pete Rose, American Hero, said some dirty words. There were cameras all around him. He didn't know one was live. Ah, the magic of television.

I know some of the words Pete Rose said. Randy Donaldson of the Braves staff told me. Obviously, I can't print any of them here, but one has four letters and the other two have seven.

One of the other two may be hyphenated, come to think of it.

Spelling dirty words can be a tricky business, because most of them aren't in the dictionary. It's anybody's guess.

What we use in the newspaper for dirty words people say is "bleep." Using "bleep" shows how the influence of the electronic media is even slipping into real journalism.

When Johnny Carson says a dirty word on television, you don't hear the dirty word, you hear an electronic sound that goes, "Bleep." Ah, the magic of television.

Wednesday, I was reading one of the local sportswriters' stories from the Rose interview. He quoted Pete as saying to Atlanta pitcher, Larry McWilliams, who robbed him of a base hit with a grand catch, "Why the hell did you catch that bleep-bleep ball?"

"Hell" is now OK in the newspaper. It is finally off the bleep list, in other words. Calling it a "bleep-bleep" ball also seems to indicate my earlier suspicions were correct. "Bleep-bleep" must be a hyphenated dirty word.

The sportswriter also quoted Rose as saying to all the sportswriters Tuesday night, "I'm going to miss you bleeps."

That bleep is no mystery to me at all. I know what ballplayers call sportswriters. Once, a ballplayer said to me, "You bleeping bleep, get your bleeping bleep away from my locker, or I'm going to knock the bleep out of you, and you can print that in your bleeping newspaper, and I don't give a bleep if you bleeping do."

I ran for the door. To save my bleep.

I am sure there were viewers Tuesday night offended by Rose's language. I just hope nobody was surprised that a big league baseball player curses. Cursing is a part of the game. Like spitting tobacco juice, scratching and adjusting, and becoming a free agent.

The first curse word I ever heard was at a baseball game. We chose up sides in the second grade and my team's first baseman, a fat boy named Roy who should have been in the fifth-grade game, chased a foul ball. He stumbled into a gully where there were many briars.

"Bleep!" he said as he picked the briars from his bleep, which was sore for a week.

The only thing Pete Rose said Tuesday night that surprised me was his expression of displeasure that the Braves' Gene Garber would pitch to him in the ninth inning "like it was the seventh game of the World Series."

What did Rose expect from a professional like Garber? Gene Garber pitches like Pete Rose bats. With the intensity of a runaway locomotive. Would Rose have eased up had it been Garber going for some sort of pitching record?

I know a word worse than any Pete Rose used on television Tuesday night. As much as I admire the man, I insist it must be applied to his remarks concerning Garber.

It has four letters, too.

B-U-S-H.

Scooter T. Washington: Blue Chipper

It was all over the Sunday paper about the recruiting of young athletes to play football at large universities in the region. It's that season. Children are snatched away from their mothers' arms back home in Twobit County and the next thing you know, the Head Coach is saying, "Ol' Dram Bowie from down in Twobit County is the finest prospect since Jiggy Smaha." Which brings up that musical question, has anybody seen Jiggy Smaha lately?

Recruiting *is* important. "You gotta have the horses," a coach once told me, "before you can pull the wagon." Coaches talk like that. Translated, it means if he doesn't get off his tail and sign some talent, he'll be selling tires at K-Mart the next time toe meets leather.

What I hear is that Tennessee is making a big move into Georgia this year in search of recruits to rebuild the once-mighty Volunteer program. You don't *sign* to go to Knoxville. You are sentenced there. Clemson is also usually heavy into seeking Georgia material. A Clemson raid especially makes Georgia Tech people mad.

"You know that tractorcade this weekend?" one asked me.

"They weren't farmers," he said. "They were Clemson fans on their way to Sears to buy clothes for the Gator Bowl."

From the various sources around the Southeast, I have come into possession of the list of the most-wanted high school athletes in the state. None have been signed yet. They are known as "blue-chippers" to the alumni. Coaches call them "job-savers." Here's the list.

ARDELL GROVER—Linebacker from Atlanta. Missed half his senior season with terminal acne. "He'll hit you," say the recruiters. Especially if you call him "Zit Head," which a tenth-grader did shortly before Ardell rendered him unconscious during fifth-period study hall.

MARVIN PALAFOX—Marvin is a tight end. He's from Macon. Wears No. 82. Scored same number on his college boards. "Great hands," say the coaches. So do the cheerleaders.

SCOOTER T. WASHINGTON—Half-back from Savannah. Olympic speed. Expensive tastes. Wants two Cadillacs and a mink coat like Reggie Jackson's to sign. Answers the telephone, "You need the loot to get the Scoot." Contact through his agent Sam the Fly at the Wise Owl Pool and Recreation Hall, Savannah.

BILLY BOB WALTON—Offensive tackle from Moultrie. Extremely offensive. Friends call him "Dump Truck" because that's how big he is and he could eat all the pork chops and mashed potatoes out of the back of one. Made *Tifton Gazette* All-Area team. Makes Junior Samples look like David Niven. Loves buttermilk, but can't spell it.

LAVONNE (The Rolling Stone) LARUE—Led Columbus school in interceptions. Also led burglary ring to back entrance of Harry's One-Stop Stereo Shop. Got one-to-five, but sentence suspended when entire student body turned out as character witnesses after suggestion they do so by several of The Stone's "acquaintances."

"Can start for any college team in the country," says his coach, who didn't start him once and still carries the scars.

IRVING BOATRIGHT III—Quarterback for a fashionable northside Atlanta private school. Father prominent Atlanta attorney with homes on Hilton Head and Sea Island. Can't play a lick, but the head coach gets free legal advice and either house three weeks each summer. Started every game during high school career. Bed-wetter.

BARTHANATOMAY RIMJOB—Place-kicker. Son of Pakistani professor of Eastern philosophy at Clayton Junior College. Kicks soccer style. Made 110 straight extra points during prep career. Does not speak English and goes through fifteen-minute ancient ritual before every kick. Weighs ninety pounds soaking wet. Once scored winning touchdown on fake field goal by hiding ball in his turban.

ALBERT WARTZ JR.—From South Georgia. 6-4, 250. Plays quarterback. Questionable student. Thinks Henry Cabot Lodge is a motel in Bainbridge. Filled out recruiting questionnaire. By "sex," wrote: "Not since Mavis Wilson moved out of Hahira."

"This kid," say his high school coach, "doesn't know the meaning of 'quit.' " Doesn't know the meaning of third-grade arithmetic either. Leaning toward Alabama.

Super Girls

NEW ORLEANS — Actually, the Dallas Cowboys cheerleaders wear a lot of clothes, comparatively speaking. Seen *Sports Illustrated's* annual porno issue this week? The cover is a lovely Brazilian child named Maria Joao, who is on the beach in Bahia. She is not naked, but you have to look closely to see that she isn't.

Inside the magazine, which is usually reserved for pictures of huge men perspiring in the name of sport, are more pictures of Maria and other Brazilian girls, all of whom would make a good man leave home for south of the border. I was especially impressed by a photograph of the same Maria Joao posing in much less than what underpants used to be in a fruit stand in Itapoa. Yes, she has some bananas.

Sports gets sexy ocassionally. *High Society,* which makes Larry Flynt's *Hustler* look like *National Geographic,* is out with a picture spread (a bad choice of words) of girls cavorting in hockey uniforms. We recently went through the annual girl-in-the-dorm story with Arkansas. Jim Bouton's *Ball Four* was a study in major league voyuerism and the lastest rumor is San Francisco leads all leagues in homosexual athletes. What more do you expect from the gay bay?

It is the Cowboys cheerleaders in their white hot pants and short halters, however, who currently rank first in sporting sensuality. Who cares if Roger Staubach will occasionally run out of the pocket? He doesn't even shave his legs. If he played in San Francisco he might, but that is beside the point.

There are thirty-two of them. The *Dallas Cowboys Weekly*, a publication sponsored by the team that will play the Denver Broncos here Sunday in Super Bowl XII, calls them "luscious lovelies." I'll hit some highlights:

There is Cheri Jo Adams. Have mercy. There is Monica Muehlhause. There ought to be a law. There is Debbie and Charyl and Connie and Lisa and Janice Garner, I think I love you.

Some of the other National Football League teams have tried to start their own cheerleading corps. Chicago has the Honey Bears. It's too cold in Chicago to show your navel after Labor Day. Curt Mosher, who was instrumental in founding the Cowboy cheerers, started the Atlanta Falconettes this past season. Get the hook. Denver has the Bronco Belles. They will compete sideline-to-sideline with the Cowboy cheerleaders here Sunday. I'm giving the Cowboy cheerleaders and three wiggles.

Steve Perkins is editor of *Dallas Cowboys Weekly* which has over 40,000 circulation. Each week of the season, the paper features a centerfold of one of the Cowboy cheerleaders. That is the main reason circulation is over 40,000.

"There were times," a Dallas man was saying, "when the pictures really got risque. Perkins didn't want to run them, but Tex Schramm (Cowboys president) said go ahead."

Perkins is here for the Super Bowl. The cheerleaders will be in Sunday. Perkins gives Schramm the credit for the cheerleaders' success and popularity. Watch a Dallas game and see the cheerleaders in action between almost every play. Television cameramen are no dummies.

"What Tex wants," says Perkins, "Tex gets. He demands the best in everything. He gets the right girls. He doesn't take any chances on them if he thinks they might cause a scandal."

So far, so good. Many of the cheerleaders are students. There are also legal secretaries, even a check-out girl at a supermarket. Some are married. There has been only one near-miss in the problem department.

A well-endowed young lady walked into a Corpus Christi topless bar recently and told the owner she was a Cowboy cheerleader and she was available for duty. The owner broke his neck getting an advertisement into the local newspaper. Schramm got wind of the hoax and informed the owner his new talent was no cheerleader. The show was cancelled.

Nearly 700 girls showed up for tryouts in Dallas last year. Those chosen are paid $15 per game. They are choreographed by a lady named, appropriately enough, Texi Waterman. The big bucks come later for personal appearances.

"It's a very lucrative situation for them," Perkins explained. "They might get $200 to go to San Antonio for the opening of an auto dealership. Five went to Little Rock the other day to open a store. They come from all over to try out. If a girl from Houston, say, makes the squad, she'll just move to Dallas.

The hottest-selling poster in the country pictures the Cowboy girls. The same photograph adorns T-shirts. They are on sale throughout the New Orleans French Quarter. Farrah in her wet suit is now a distant second. The first twenty days the posters were on the market, sales reached 20,000.

A number of questions remain concerning the Dallas darlings:

Do any of the players date cheerleaders?

Randy White rolled out of bounds late in a Dallas rout and asked one of the girls to dinner. She accepted.

Do any of the cheerleaders also have brains? Vanessa Baker, a six-year veteran, was recently awarded her master's degree in education from Texas Woman's University. She made all A's.

How can I get a Dallas Cowboy cheerleader of my very own?

A man from Hollywood called one of the cheerleaders last year and told her he had seen her on television and she was beautiful and he wanted to give her a screen test.

She went to see him. Not once, but twice, and then a third time. The last time, the man was no longer with the studio. He was fired for flying a Dallas Cowboy cheerleader to California three times when there were no jobs available at the studio.

Lest We Forget

For the past two weekends, the Falcons, Flames, Hawks, Techs, and Georgias have all been winners, and Losersville is surely dead they say. What miracles next? Wyman C. Lowe winning an election? MARTA making a friend?

In New York, they celebrate winning the World Series. Dallas holds the Super Bowl trophy. Even tiny Green Bay rejoices. It leads the league again. Here, we celebrate winning weedends. Atlanta is a sports cancer patient that just got the word its head cold is clearing up.

But forgive us our headiness over what others might consider routine. Little things mean a lot when the suffering has been long and constant.

Georgia Tech people are talking about a bowl game. Georgia's football team—and we can claim it as being at least "local"—was supposed to embarrass the basketball squad. Now, it has a chance to win the Southeastern Conference title.

A Falcon placekicker actually attempted a field goal in the waning moments of a game and made it for victory. The basketball Hawks defeated powerful Denver. And the Flames defeated Montreal in hockey. That's impossible. Montreal invented ice.

Sound the trumpets for the lame and downtrodden. A Polish boy has grown up to be pope, and Atlanta may be slowly rising from the ashes of athletic ruin.

(The only words of caution I might offer are not to forget that the Braves open spring training in just five months, and you remember what happened to the last pope.)

But before the seedy and checkered past of Atlanta sports is dumped into history's garbage pile, I would like to recall briefly a few of the dumpees. We simply cannot say goodbye to Losersville that quickly.

Not without at least a mention of some of our classic losers and the moments they gave us:

—— In the final game of the 1972 season, Falcon running-back Dave Hampton became the first player in the team's history to gain over 1,000 yards in a season. Play was stopped, and he was awarded the game ball. On the next snap, Hampton was thrown for a big loss and time ran out before he could regain the lost 1,000th.

—— In his first major league game, Braves' rookie shortstop Leo Foster booted the first ground ball hit to him. In his first major league at-bat, he hit into a triple play.

—— How did Losersville maintain itself year after year? Here are some of the names of Number One draft choices of Atlanta professional teams:

Skip Harlika, Gerald Tinker, Ron Broaddus, Tom Workman, John Small, Greg Marx, John Valleley, Joe Profit, Gene Hobart, George Trapp and Leo Carroll.

Of that group, Leo Carroll is the most notable. Drafted by the Falcons to improve their offensive line, he disappeared one night from training camp.

All he left was his Tiny Tim "Tiptoe Through the Tulips" record.

—— Early in their history, the Flames launched an ad campaign warning fans all season tickets would soon be gone, the demand being so great. A few years later, management was begging city leaders for donations to help meet the team payroll.

—— The closest the Falcons ever came to making the playoffs was in 1973. They won seven straight, but then collapsed and lost back-to-back to Buffalo and St. Louis to be eliminated from post-season play.

The head coach, Norman Van Brocklin, blamed it all on "Peachtree Street whores and bartenders."

——In the middle of a thirteen-game losing streak, the Braves' team bus got lost in the middle of a swamp between the airport and downtown in Philadelphia.

——Great Trades Number One: The Falcons gave Minnesota their top quarterback, Bob Berry, and their top draft choice for the coming year in return for the Vikings' number two linebacker, Lonnie Warwick, and number two quarterback, Bob Lee. The Vikings later used the draft choice to obtain a player named Chuck Foreman.

—— Great Trades Number Two: The Hawks gave Pete Maravich to the New Orleans Jazz.

—— For opening game 1977 the Braves asked Bert Lance to throw out the first ball. He was stuck in a stadium elevator for thirty minutes and finished the season lower than the pitiable team he had launched.

—— Falcons' quarterback Randy Johnson, sacked several times this given Sunday, led his team out of the huddle and lined up behind a guard.

—— That's nothing. Falcon fullback Art Malone and tight end Jim Mitchell went into an Atlanta huddle and got into a fistfight before the next play could be called.

—— Georgia Tech's 1971 football team was invited to the Peach Bowl, but voted not to go, much to the relief of head coach Bud Carson. Athletic officials demanded that another vote be taken, however, and the pressured players this time voted "yes."

Tech lost the game 41-18 in the mud and Carson got fired.

—— The first Falcons game ever was an exhibition at the Stadium against Philadelphia in 1966. The Falcons were to kick off to launch themselves into the National Football League.

The whistle blew and kicker Wade Traynam approached the ball.

He whiffed it.

Third Down and Praise the Lord

A few years ago, I talked to a wonderful preacher named William Holmes Borders, pastor of the Wheat Street Baptist Church, about the political problems Atlanta was having at the time.

The conversation was background work for a series The *Atlanta Constitution* produced called "City in Crisis." A lot of people didn't like what "City in Crisis" said. It said Atlanta had polarized politically, our leaders were more interested in bickering than progressing, and the City Too Busy To Hate was growing ornery.

What I remember most about that conversation was William Holmes Borders saying, "What we need in this city more than anything else is for our sports teams to get off their behinds and give us something to cheer. The Lord willing, maybe someday they will."

"The Lord willing . . ." is the key phrase here. I will be the first to admit the recent rise to prominence of our local sporting heroes is nothing short of miraculous, but never have I heard so much credit given to Providence for athletic success.

Take the Falcons. The Falcons have seven victories and only four losses, and Sunday in New Orleans, the tipped-pass-for-a-touchdown that defeated the Saints in the final seconds was hailed by one reporter as the "Immaculate Reception."

The phraseology is superb. The man who threw the ball, oft-injured and maligned Steve Bartkowski, makes Lazarus look like an amateur. He has risen time and again from the quarterbacking graveyard, and he has also announced he has been "born again."

Another writer wondered, "Now that he has found the Lord, will he be able to find his secondary receivers?"

Here is what Steve Bartkowski said Sunday after his prayerful pass was answered:

"I just said, 'Praise the Lord.' He was with us. I was praying real hard."

You would think if anybody was going to get help from Above, it would have been the Saints, who are named for those with, I would imagine, heavy influence when it comes to heavenly decisions.

I don't know how much the Flames figure God has had to do with their resurrection. It wasn't that long ago there was talk of the franchise going broke, but now the Great Goalie in the Sky is certainly smiling down on Omni center ice.

Last time I looked, the Hawks were only a game behind in their division. Holy turnover! Sadly, the only team yet to be saved from the fiery depths of the league cellar is the Braves. Let's all stand and sing the first and last verses of "Just As I Am."

Even our collegiate athletes are in the spirit. Just about the time I had decided Vince Dooley had sold out to the devil for his Georgia team's incredible 8-1 season, I find out the Bulldog quarterback, Jeff Pyburn, has linked up with the Almighty.

And recall what happened a few weeks back when Georgia played Kentucky. Kentucky led 16-0 in the third quarter. But with seconds to play, there stood kicker Rex Robinson with a field-goal attempt to win the game.

"I just put my faith in the Lord," Robinson said after the kick was good, "and He blessed me."

Eddie Lee Ivery, the Georgia Tech running back who set an NCAA single-game rushing record against Air Force Saturday? He's deeply religious and occassionally offers a locker-room sermon.

And to think Atlanta used to have athletes like Alex Hawkins, the former Falcons receiver, who, admittedly, once made the Fellowship of Christian Athletes' all-opponent team.

I certainly don't want to cast aspersions on other people's faith—athletes included—but I do sort of wonder what with the Middle East (which is sort of God's home town), starvation, crime, and discos, does He really have time to bless a field goal or a touchdown pass?

Since I couldn't get a direct interview, I can only speculate the answer would probably be: Only when it is absolutely necessary. Like when Notre Dame is playing for the national championship.

The best religion-in-sports story I know is an old one, but one I would suggest every athlete and fan who thinks God gives an angel's feather about third-and-long should hear again.

A spectator at a boxing match was sitting next to a priest. When the bell rang, one of the fighters crossed himself before heading to the middle of the ring.

"Will that help him, Father?" asked the spectator.

"Not if he can't fight," said the priest.

Dwayne Sanders

DURHAM, N.C. — On September 9, 1978—a sweltering, late summer Saturday—Duke and Georgia Tech played a game of college football in a tattered, half-empty stadium named after an old coach.

Georgia Tech will remember the occasion as a nightmare, its second, thanks to Duke, in less than a year.

The Tech sidelines, as the end drew near, was an outdoor death row. Men and boys, condemned to bitter and solid defeat, cursed themselves, cursed the officials, and cursed the heat. Mostly, they cursed the heat.

A giant Tech lineman, his body bloody and drenched in sweat, looked toward the sky and spat at the sun.

Football, when you are losing, is a game of reassurance. We are surrounded by a million Indians, but any minute now the Cavalry will appear and the day will be saved. Sure, it will.

"We'll win it," said a Tech assistant at halftime, the score 10-3 in favor of Duke. "I can feel it."

"The second half," added a player, "belongs to us."

There was agreement all about. But help never came. The bugles never blew. And the heat—damn the heat—grew worse, completing the agony.

September 9, 1978: Duke 28, Georgia Tech 10.

Remember the day, if you favor the White and Gold, as an ungodly day of frustration.

Then, forget it. And put your mind to the misfortune of a young man who had a stinking Saturday, too.

His loss was worse than any silly football game ever played. As Duke was kicking Georgia Tech Saturday afternoon, he was in the Duke University Hospital fighting for the use of the bottom two-thirds of his body.

It happened shortly before the game began. Dwayne Sanders, who is eighteen, was warming up with his fellow Georgia Tech cheerleaders.

It was to be his first game as a cheerleader. He's a sophomore at Tech. "About the hardest worker we got," said one of his partners.

Dwayne Sanders, from Atlanta's Henderson High School, did a few flips on the trampoline in front of the Tech supporters.

Then, he did one more. The kickoff was near. The bands were playing, balloons filled the air. Duke was worrying about the running of Eddie Lee Ivery. Tech was worrying about the passing of Stanley Driskell.

"He made the flip okay," a Tech cheerleader explained it, "but when he did his roll coming out, that's when he got hurt."

It took the ambulance a half hour to arrive. Dwayne Sanders lay on the grass, unable to move the bottom portion of his body.

His neck was broken. His removal from the field was barely noticed. The remaining Tech cheerleaders gave him a good-luck cheer.

At this writing, Dwayne Sanders was in intensive care at the Duke Hospital. He was to undergo diagnostic surgery. A doctor explained:

"It's too early to know what the outcome will be. Depending on the swelling and the pressure, he could regain his movement. It was a freak thing. The only thing you can do is hope."

The doctor crossed both his fingers.

Another doctor said, "Had the injury been higher, it could have been fatal."

So scream if you will about Georgia Tech's football ineptness Saturday. Granted, the defense leaked. And the offense proved why Pepper Rodgers doesn't like the forward pass. And there were questionable calls by the officals at times. "Welcome to the Atlantic Coast Conference," somebody said.

And, of course, focus the blame for it all squarely upon the shoulders of the head coach, for that is the American way of losing.

But do it quickly and then get along to concern for Dwayne Sanders. There will be other Saturdays and other chances for Tech's football team. Believe it or not at this point, there will even be times to praise it.

On such occassions, may Dwayne Sanders, the Lord willing, be there to lead the cheers.

(Dwayne Sanders did not recover. He remains confined to a wheelchair.)

Baseball's Spittin' Image

Watching baseball on television offers a rare opportunity to see the players up close. The Big Eye can put you nose-to-nose with your favorite stars, most of whom apparently do not shave on a regular basis.

Thurman Munson of the Yankees, for instance, looks like Pancho Villa after a two-week binge. Davy Lopes of the Dodgers looks like the guy who waters his horse.

The reason television has so much time to show closeup shots of the players during a game is there is a lot of standing around in baseball. Baseball is the only sport where three-fourths of the game is a time out.

Here comes the batter towards the plate. Watch him take a few practice swings, knock the dirt out of his spikes, fondle the tar rag, and scratch and adjust. (When a game is on national television, players should be reminded to cut down on the scratching and adjusting.)

There stands the pitcher on the mound. Watch him tug at his cap, pound the ball in the glove, pick up the resin bag, throw it down again, lean over for the sign, shake it off, nod agreement to the next one, and then throw over to first.

The batter steps out and here we go again, more practice swinging, dirt-knocking, and, if you must know, more scratching and adjusting.

Television even goes into the dugouts now. Dugouts used to be off-limits to civilians. A player could scratch and adjust and yawn and figure tax shelters until the last man was out, and who would know?

"Now," a ballplayer told me, "you have to act interested in the game for nine full innings."

Seeing the players up close on television during this year's Yankees-Dodgers World Series has also brought to my attention another interesting thing about men who play baseball for a living.

They spit more than anybody else. I don't suppose they spit on each other that much, but they spit on everything else. Home plate. The bases. The on-deck circle. Their hands. They used to spit on the ball, but that was outlawed. Leo Durocher once spit on an umpire.

Many baseball players chew tobacco. They all look like they have cheek tumors, but at least you expect them to spit. God help them if they didn't.

But watching the World Series games, I've noticed even baseball players who chew nothing at all also spit a lot.

Take Reggie Jackson of the Yankees. He spits constantly, even when he is figuring tax shelters in the dugout. He spits walking to the plate. He spits while he is there. He spits on balls. He spits on strikes.

Reggie Jackson spits with style. He has two distinct spits. There is the straight "ptui!" spit where he simply applies cheek and lip pressure.

His deluxe, superstar spit—typically flamboyant—is his through-the-teeth-line-drive-spit, however. He can fire away five to ten quick streams through the gap in his two front teeth faster than a Ron Guidry fastball.

One of the advantages to playing major-league baseball, I suppose, is it is one of the few professions that allows you to spit on national television and not be considered uncouth.

Other professional athletes don't have that luxury. Imagine Jack Nicklaus walking away from a putt on the scenic sixteenth green at Augusta and spitting. Basketball players wouldn't spit on a shiny hardwood floor. Hockey players might spit on the ice if they had more teeth. Jockeys don't spit during horse races out of concern for their fellow riders to the rear.

A private citizen certainly can't spit in public. It is considered nasty, and it could spread disease. It's like a New Yorker mentioned to me recently.

"Strange thing about the subways in New York," he said. "You spit and they fine you $25, but you can throw up for nothing."

I really don't have anything against baseball players spitting. Maybe what bothers me is television insists upon showing them doing it close up.

Then, again, perhaps I should count my blessings. Television has gone face-to-face with the players and into their dugouts today. Tomorrow, the showers?

Georgia 28, Georgia Tech 28

ATHENS — I was totally biased about the Georgia-Georgia Tech football game they played here Saturday. I admit it. Openly, and without shame. None of that I'm-just-here-to-report-the-facts nonsense for me.

I wanted a tie, dammit. When Georgia scored a touchdown in the waning moments to make the score 28-27 in favor of Georgia Tech, I hoped Bulldog Coach Vince Dooley would momentarily lose hold of his faculties and go for a one-point conversion.

It's happened to him before. Just two weeks ago in Auburn.

Why should anybody have to lose a game like this? A tie at Auburn cost Georgia the Southeastern Conference title and the Sugar Bowl trip.

A tie Saturday, and neither Tech nor Georgia would have suffered the slightest pain. The Yellow Jackets would still have had their Peach Bowl bid, and the Bulldogs would have kept their date in Houston's Bluebonnet, and ABC would still have had the hit of their collegiate telecast season.

Tech-Georgia 1978 was more than a game. It was a spectacle. A classic. One team, Georgia Tech, builds an early lead. Twenty-to-nothing. But the other team, Georgia, fights back and with the stadium falling in, scores to lead 21-20.

But Georgia Tech won't hold, either. Drew Hill runs the kickoff back 102 yards for a touchdown, and the score is 28-21. ABC should double its payment to both schools for the right to show the rest of the nation such a show.

It isn't over. Here come the Bulldogs behind a boy-child quarterback named Buck Belue. And Georgia scores. Twenty-eight-to-twenty-seven. Two minutes, twenty-four seconds remaining.

Of course, Vince Dooley went for the two points and the victory. And his people in red were successful in the attempt, and despite what I thought, somebody did have to lose Saturday—Georgia Tech.

Twenty-nine to twenty-eight.

"It was the best Tech-Georgia game I have ever seen," said Georgia publicist and historian, Dan Magill.

Georgia celebrated into the dusk. There is something Bulldog fans say at a time like this. They say, "How bout them Dawgs?", a grammatical insult, but it gets the point across.

There is something Georgia Tech people say at a time like this too, and player after player was saying it in the Tech dressing quarters after the game. That's as far as I will go. Use your imagination.

I had rather be a brain surgeon than a big-time college football coach. There's less pressure. Lose in brain surgery, and you can say you did your best, and you still get paid.

"What are they doing over on the winner's side?", asked Pepper

Rodgers, a big-time college football coach who wished he had chosen another line of work after the heartbreak of Saturday.

The Tech players were stunned. They sat there, staring at nothing, slowly pulling off equipment and tossing it into a heap of tape and bloodied jerseys on the floor.

I've been to funerals more lively. And speaking of funerals, Rodgers did: "This is like a death in the family," he said.

"I want it to hurt! I want it to hurt!" a Georgia fan, flowing in the spirit, said to the Tech team as it filed off the field. He got his wish.

Georgia was brilliant in its comeback. And credit the Bulldog faithful. At 20-0, Tech, they were still on their feet, beseeching their team to recover from enough early mistakes to lose five games. The crowd was worth at least a touchdown.

And Georgia Tech was so close. Had Eddie Lee Ivery, the best player on the field, not been injured in the second half, the Jackets would have likely been able to hold their lead that vanished at the eleventh hour.

"It was like losing a tennis match when the last shot hits the tape," said Rodgers.

There is something both sides should remember after the events of Saturday. It's something a Georgia man said to me once.

It was a dozen years ago, and I was talking to Bulldog lineman John Kasay, now a Dooley assistant. Georgia had won a big game. The Bulldog dressing room was New Year's Eve.

But John Kasay looked around him and put the moment in its proper perspective.

"Why is it," he asked, "the highs are never as high as the lows are low?"

There is another way to put it. Losing hurts worse than winning feels good.

A tie, dammit. Georgia 28. Georgia Tech 28. Everybody shake hands and go home happy.

Larry Munson: Better Than Being There

Sometime in the wee hours of Sunday morning, my telephone rang. Even the ring sounded drunk. Among a number of other bad things, alcohol in large quantities dulls the ability of the user to tell time.

I muttered a groggy, hesitant, "Hello?"

"Gooooooo Daaaawgs!" was the reply from the other end. Deliver me from Billy Bulldog when it's the middle of the night, Georgia won, and the whiskey hasn't run out.

"That you, Dorsey?" I asked. It had to be. It had to be Dorsey Hill, the world's biggest Bulldog fan. Dorsey Hill thinks when you die you go to Vince Dooley's house. He can't wait.

Last year, when Georgia lost to Kentucky, 33-0, Dorsey claimed it didn't count because Kentucky was on probation for recruiting violations and had too many players from New Jersey.

"Best team money could buy," is how he described the victorious Wildcats, who went on to tie for the Southeastern Conference title. Dorsey dies hard.

I was awake enough by now to realize why the telephone call. Only hours before, Georgia had avenged last season's loss to Kentucky with a thrilling 17-16 victory in Lexington. The Bulldogs had trailed 16-0 in the third quarter.

"I never gave up," Dorsey said. "After the miracle at Grant Field Saturday, I knew the Lord would give us one, too."

He was referring to Georgia Tech's equally thrilling 17-13 defeat of Florida Saturday afternoon. Dorsey doesn't like Georgia Tech or anybody who does.

"I like it when we sweep a double-header," he explains. "That's when Georgia wins and Tech loses."

I have never quite understood that thinking, but there are those among the Georgia Tech followers who feel the same about the Bulldogs.

"I wouldn't pull for Georgia," a Tech man once told me, "with one engine out on the team plane."

I thought Saturday was one of the grandest days in Georgia collegiate football history. Tech wins its sixth straight and Grant Field hasn't been that full of life in years. That old house on North Avenue literally trembled with delight when Eddie Lee Ivery scored the Yellow Jackets' winning touchdown.

And Georgia's drive to the Rex Robinson field goal in the final moments was a classic profile in sporting courage. Georgia is only two victories—Florida and Auburn—away from another SEC championship and a trip to the Sugar Bowl. That is astounding when you consider that in the pre-season, the Bulldogs bore a strong resemblance to Vanderbilt.

I am almost frightened to consider the ramifications of a Falcons' victory over the Rams Monday night at the Stadium. If the clinkers win, close the schools and banks and I demand a parade.

There was one other hero Saturday besides the Eddie Lee Iverys, the Willie McClendons and the Rex Robinsons. He is a fiftyish fellow from Minnesota.

He worked in Wyoming for a time, and then spent years and years in Nashville. He moved to Atlanta only a few months ago, but he is one of us now.

"The traffic here," he says, "is murder."

Larry Munson has been broadcasting Georgia football games for thirteen years. Saturday night was his finest hour. His description of the closing moments of the Georgia-Kentucky game, said a man listening with me, "is Bobby Thomson's home run against the Dodgers all over again."

It was so good, the Sunday paper reprinted Munson's call of the winning Georgia field goal word-for-word.

"It's set down, it looks good—watch it! YEAH! YEAH! YEAH! YEAH! Three seconds left! Rex Robinson put 'em ahead, 17-16!"

It was so good, Dorsey Hill said, "listening to Larry Munson was better than being there."

Frame that one, Larry. There is no higher praise.

Two Little Girls

Two little girls went out to play in the sun one day. One wore a pretty yellow dress. She was tall, and she wore her hair in a pigtail.

The other little girl wore blue shorts. She was shorter, and her hair was red. She had many freckles.

It was very hot this day.

"What should we play?" asked the little girl with the pigtail.

"How about tennis?" said the little girl with red hair.

"That sounds like fun," said her friend. "I'll serve."

The two little girls played tennis for a long, long time.

The little girl with the pigtail won the first five games. Her friend won the sixth game, but soon the first set was over. The score was 6-1.

The little girl with red hair played much better the second set and won by the same score. Six games to one.

"Let's play one more," she said.

"I'll serve," said her friend.

The two little girls played on and on. The redheaded girl led 2-0. Then, she lost three straight games. The score became 5-5. Golly, what a neato match. Back and forth and back and forth went the tennis balls. There were crosscourt backhands and down-the-line forehands. There were deep lobs and excellent gets and much topspin.

One time, the little girl with red hair had a match point against her. She hit a drop-shot winner. Jimmy Conners wouldn't try a drop-shot winner facing a match point.

The little girl with the red hair was not old enough to know better.

It was very exciting, but suddenly the two little girls weren't having as much fun as they thought they would. So tense was the little girl with the pigtail, she began to cry after missing an easy shot.

She cried and she cried, and she stomped her foot and she contorted her face into an awful shape.

The little girl with red hair did not cry, but when she missed a shot, it hurt her very badly. Once, she hit herself on the head with her racquet because she missed a shot.

"Dummy," she muttered to herself.

By this time, the little girls were covered in perspiration and their cute play outfits were soaking wet.

The sun beat down on them ferociously during the final game. The little girl with red hair was leading 6-5, serving for the match.

She had three match points, but each time the little girl with the pigtail sent the game back to duece. The little girl with the pigtail cried between almost every point.

"I wish we had decided to play something else," she thought to herself.

Suddenly, it was over. The little girl with the pigtail hit a backhand over the baseline. She said, "Nice match" to her friend and then she cried some more.

Many people had gathered to watch the two little girls play tennis because they played so well. "There is probably a quarter of a million dollars worth of lessons between them," said a man.

Other men made wagers on the outcome of the tennis match between the two little girls who will probably grow up to be millionairesses.

The two little girls each received a silver dish for playing so well. The little girl with the red hair got a bigger dish because she won the match.

Her name was Margaret Hopkins, and she lives in Illinois. Her friend was Cari Hagey. She lives in California. They played at the Bitsy Grant Tennis Center in Atlanta.

Margaret Hopkins, because she beat Cari Hagey, is now the top-ranked twelve-year-old girl tennis player in all of the nation. When the match was over, she smiled and showed her braces.

It was the first time either of the two little girls had smiled in over two hours.

Wow. Tennis is such fun.

Eighty-Pound Lawsuit

I have always been a bit skeptical about organized athletics for children not old enough to have all their permanent teeth.

What is it about a society that will put a bat in the hand of a six-year-old, dress him in a baseball uniform, and ask him to perform on a diamond with real bases and everything, including umpires, coaches, and shouting spectators?

There is something called the "T-League." That's for kids who have just graduated from potty training. How can a child who hasn't learned his ABCs yet be expected to know to hit the cutoff man?

In the T-League, there is no pitcher. The ball is placed on a tee at the plate and the batter takes his cuts. Once I saw a T-League game where there was a close play at the plate. The runner was called out.

The runner's coach disputed the call. A grown man who would argue with an umpire at a baseball game involving toddlers is a sick person.

As the rhubarb continued, the opposing team's centerfielder became bored with the proceedings. He took off his glove, sat down in the outfield and began playing in the sand next to the fence.

Now, the other coach came storming out of his dugout. "Johnny!" he screamed to the youngster. "Do you want to play baseball, son?"

The child, still engrossed in the sand, studied his coach's inquiry for a moment, and then answered him by shaking his head, "No." Sand is marvelous when you are six, but it's lonely in centerfield.

I read an incredible story in the newspaper the other day about children playing organized athletics. It happened in Cobb County. Two midget football teams, nine-to-eleven year olds, play a game Saturday that ended in an 8-8 tie.

The winner would have gone on to the league playoffs that lead to an eventual "Super Bowl" championship. I am convinced adults organize children's athletic teams for their own enjoyment and glorification. Otherwise, who would care which team of nine-to-eleven year olds would emerge as champions over other teams of nine-to-eleven olds?

Since the game ended in a tie, neither team qualified for more play. Wait until next year, and let's all go home and play with the dog.

But, first, let's file a lawsuit.

Adults involved with the Mableton team claimed the other team, South Cobb, had hired its own officials for the game and had not gone by rules stating officials should be named by something called the Cobb County Midget Football Conference.

They wanted the game played over. They filed a protest to the conference. Protest denied. They hired an attorney. He asked a Superior Court judge to stop the playoffs until the matter could be settled.

"When you set up an organization, you say you are going to go by the rules," attorney for the plaintiff, Laurie Davis, told me. "But when there is a clear violation and nobody will listen to you, where do you go?

"Do you have a fistfight to settle it? No, you try to find somebody who will listen and make a fair decision."

That is Laurie Davis' explanation of why an issue involving eighty-pound football players was taken to court.

Good for Judge Luther Hames. Why he even agreed to hear the case is a puzzle, but at least he denied the request to stop the league playoffs and found there was no reason whatsoever for the court to get involved further.

Why not let children be children while they have the chance? Whatever happened to games where you chose sides and played in the yard and made up your own rules and never invited the overgrown kid across the street because he could hit the ball too far?

Whatever happened to damming creeks and climbing trees and playing in mud and marbles?

And what do you tell your ten-year-old son, the quarterback, when he asks, "Hey, dad, what's a lawsuit?"

Gatewood Dooper at the Masters

AUGUSTA — The press corps that covers the Masters at Augusta National ranks just above the guys with the pointed sticks who go around the course picking up paper "the best gallery in golf" strews from Flowering Paranoia to Blooming Threeputtomia.

I was lucky enough this year not to qualify for a Genuine, Official, Keep-It-Pinned-on-Your-Person-at-All-Times press badge.

So I have set up shop in a tree overlooking the beautiful par-three twelfth. I have disguised myself as Tom Weiskopf having a nervous breakdown.

Tom Weiskopf is one of my favorite golfers. Last year, he shot a bad round in the Masters and stormed out of the locker room with a number of reporters in hot pursuit. He slammed the screen door that leads to the clubhouse grill with such force it knocked the frown off a Pinkerton man.

"Tommy takes a bad round hard," somebody said. They should take away his shoelaces and hide all sharp objects while Weiskopf is on the grounds.

The toughest thing about being a member of the press corps for the Masters tournament is the players' interviews. Contending players sit on a platform in the press barn while grown men from Tokyo to Tuscaloosa write down everything the golfers say concerning their day's rounds.

The fun part is when a golfer "goes over his round." Going over one's round is describing in full detail every blow struck for eighteen holes. . . .

"On number 1, I hit a driver 267 yards just to the right, hit an eight-iron twenty-three feet, six inches from the pin, etc., etc."

It is not as boring as watching wheelchair needlepoint, but it is close. I have this recurring fantasy about listening to a golfer go over his round. I know what Nicklaus did. He hit a drive down the middle 4,000 yards, hit a wedge to the stick and tapped it in with his middle finger. On 16, he walked across the water to the green after holing his tee shot. That's everyday stuff.

I want them to bring in Gatewood Dooper from the Clubfoot
Links in Oshkosh who got into the tournament by some strange
quirk of Masters eligibility fate and then played like a goat with
muscular distrophy.

Let me hear *him* go over his round with the world's press assem-
bled. Here is Gatewood Dooper describing his 107, worst round in
Masters history:

"On the first tee, I wet my pants. That's a two-stroke penalty
and very embarrassing. I was hitting three on my opening drive. It
landed in a trap. I wound up with a nine. My wife went back to the
car.

"On 2, I went into the trap again. The one behind number 3
green. I managed to save double bogey. My sponsor made an ob-
scene gesture and went looking for my wife.

"On 3, 4 and 5, I had bogeys. My caddy agreed to stay for one
more hole. I triple-bogeyed 6 and he went back to my car, too. To
slice my tires.

"At 7, I hit a spectator. I had to. He came at me with a rock.

"I made the turn at seventeen-over. Before I teed off on 10, the
tournament committee asked me to withdraw, my wife came back
to the course and asked me for a divorce, and my sponsor stripped
his company's name off my bag and hat.

"I fell into the lake on 12. One of the marshals pushed me. My
drive went into the crowd lining the fairway at 13. I had to take
another penalty. They hid my ball.

"Number 14 and number 15 were both disasters. At 16, they
threw beer at me. At 17, I twisted my ankle. My playing partner
tripped me. At 18, they sang 'Turkey in the Straw' while I tried to
hit out of the rough.

"After I finally putted out, they put my card in the paper shred-
der and I had to hightail it to the locker room. The tournament
committee had ordered sniper fire from the roof of Ike and
Mamie's cottage."

Tough luck, Gatewood, but hang in there. From the nearest
magnolia. Incidentally, Tommy Weiskopf usually brings extra
rope.

I Am the Wind

I have received a lot of nasty mail from joggers lately. All I said was joggers make lousy conversationalists and their feet smell bad.

Even Gayle Barron, the famous runner, agreed with me in part. "The last thing I want to talk about at a party," she told me, "is how far everybody ran that week."

Gayle Barron is the prettiest jogger I know. It's OK if her feet smell bad.

I am not against physical fitness. I am against talking about it night and day. There are too many other topics that interest me more. Like famous left-handed Chinese yacht racers.

A man from Sandy Springs finally got to me. "The reason you don't like joggers," he wrote, "is you are jealous. I'd like to see you run the Peachtree Road Race. You wouldn't make the first one hundred yards."

I can't believe he said that. I took it as a dare. Never let it be said I am the kind of man who would back down from a challenge. My boyhood friend and idol Weyman C. Wannamaker Jr., a great American, once dared me to put a dead frog down the front of Kathy Sue Loudermilk's dress in biology class.

I would have done it, too, but there was a problem. There wasn't room for anything else down the front of Kathy Sue's dress, that lovely child.

I won't run in the Peachtree race Tuesday with the 12,000 official entrants. It is a matter of principle.

Let Hal Gulliver, our editor, carry The *Constitution's* banners. Hal Gulliver, incidentally, is the perfect example of what can happen to a person who jogs. Before he started jogging, he looked like Tarzan. There was a picture of him in his running clothes in the paper. Now he looks like Jane.

I didn't want to mention it, but the smart-aleck letters have forced me to reveal I have already run the Peachtree Road Race 6.2-mile course.

I did it over the weekend. Alone. Just me, my swim suit, and a pair of slightly used jogging shoes I borrowed from my neighbor who recently gave up running.

"I had to," he explained. "My wife wouldn't run, and I didn't think we could survive a mixed marriage."

I made my run under the cloak of darkness. I wanted no publicity, no spectators, no big-name hoofers to run behind.

I departed Lenox Square from what will be Tuesday's starting line at 3 A.M. I crushed out a final cigarette, took a deep breath of the humid air and jogged away into the night.

Lonely is the nocturnal runner. The only sound was the rhythmic beat of the soles of my neighbor's jogging shoes. *Clop! Clop! Clop!* The first mile fell to its knees behind me.

Like an eagle swept through the air by some unseen current, I reached the International House of Pancakes, which was closed, still in a smooth, graceful glide.

Only an occasional passing motorist and an empty MARTA bus broke my solitude. That and a wino asleep in the entrance to an adult movie house in Buckhead and two fellows strolling on the sidewalk near West Wesley. I think they were more than pals.

I imagined myself upon a gallant steed, loping toward the dawn and the liquor store, which was also closed, at the top of the next hill.

On past Brookwood station and past Spring street. I reach Colony Square, slowing down, but still in forceful stride.

I am the wind.

I turned left on Twelfth Street, crossed Piedmont, and swept into the park. I rounded the lake and headed toward what will be Tuesday's finish line. My strength was fading, but my courage was not. Frank Shorter was on my heels. I left him in my wake.

Finally, it was over. The eagle had landed. My time is not important, for I ran not for glory. I ran simply to prove to a clod in Sandy Springs with jock itch on the brain I could conquer his silly 6.2 miles of asphalt.

Mission accomplished.

Mike Reinhardt

SHINE

WITH GLAMOUR

12 ISSUES $12

(JUST $1 EACH!)

NAME _____
(Please print)

ADDRESS _____ APT ____

CITY _____ STATE _____ ZIP _____

☐ **PAYMENT ENCLOSED**

☐ **BILL ME**

For Canada, add $13. Your first issue will be mailed within 6 weeks.

4J29

BUSINESS REPLY MAIL
FIRST CLASS PERMIT NO. 365 BOULDER, COLORADO

POSTAGE WILL BE PAID BY ADDRESSEE

GLAMOUR®

P.O. Box 51400
Boulder, Colorado 80321-1400

The Grief Passes Slowly

Billy Henderson has one of the last crew cuts in captivity. When he talks, he talks about how much he enjoys doing a job that involves young people, and there is no doubting his sincerity. Saturday is an important day in his life. In the evening, the football team he coaches, Clarke Central High School, will play Valdosta High for the state AAA championship. The game will be played in Athens.

Billy has been the full twenty yards during his career. Once he played before 73,000 people in the Sugar Bowl. Wally Butts was his coach. Georgia was his school. And he has seen the view from the other side, too. Before he moved to Clarke Central, he coached at tiny Mt. de Sales, a private school near Macon. When he went to Athens to interview, the nuns at Mt. de Sales held a mass and beseeched Providence to keep him in their fold. It was Clarke Central's prayers that were answered.

Billy took his team to Jekyll Island for its preseason training camp back in August.

Four months and thirteen games later, it is still undefeated. And it still remembers what happened on Jekyll the day it broke camp. These things are always so sudden. But the shock lingers. And the grief passes so slowly.

It was August 19, at 1:20 P.M. to be precise. Barry Malcom was sixteen. Billy Henderson, who cared for him deeply, recalls every detail.

"We were having our final lunch before heading back to Athens. Some of the players' families always come down for a few days at the beach together.

"We were about to eat when Mr. Malcom, Barry's dad, came up to me and asked if Barry could join the family. I invited him to stay for lunch. He said he'd come back later.

"After we ate, Barry left with his dad for their motel. We left for Athens. I was listening to the radio later that afternoon. The news came on. A youngster had been struck by lightning and killed on Jekyll. I froze. I was speechless. It was Barry."

Barry Malcom was a guard on the Clarke Central team. He weighed only 150 pounds. "But he would tackle a giant," said Billy Henderson. "He was a shining example."

Barry was standing outside, fifty yards from the front door of the Jekyll motel, when the bolt struck. Every effort was made to revive him. His father put him in his car and drove him into the hospital in Brunswick. At four o'clock that afternoon, he was pronounced dead.

"We drove on into Athens," the coach said. "There was the tendency to turn around and go back, but we knew there was nothing we could do. When we pulled into the parking lot at the high school, cars were lined up for blocks. They didn't know if we had heard the news."

What still hurts Billy Henderson is to talk about the Malcom family's drive back to Athens that night. "I don't know how they did it," he said. "They came all that way, with that burden, in the rain."

Life goes on. The season would open soon, against rival Cedar Shoals. "The team wanted to do something," Billy said. "They wanted to do something that was a tribute to Barry."

Barry Malcom would have worn number '65'. That number is on the top of every Clark Central player's jersey. The mothers did the sewing.

Barry Malcom's parents have seen every game this season. They will be at the field behind Clarke Central High School Saturday night for the game of the year.

"They are wonderful people," said Billy Henderson. "It's not a wealthy family, but they have stuck by us. They are a part of us."

As we talked, Billy had to choke some of the words out. Death took a favorite player. It is obvious, his coach is still taking it hard.

Thirteen years ago, he had gone through the same thing. Billy Henderson was coaching football at Willingham High in Macon. His team opened with a 21-0 victory over Warner Robins.

Monday was Labor Day. One of his players was parked at a stop sign in Macon with his girl. Somebody ran the stop sign and crashed into them. Both the player and the girl were killed.

The player was Billy Henderson's quarterback. He was also sixteen. His name was Brad. Brad Henderson, Billy's eldest son.

Boston

BOSTON — As I sit on my rump smoking cigarettes and typing this, I can still see runners coming in from the suburb of Hopkinton, 26 miles and 385 yards from the Boston Marathon finish line at the downtown Prudential Center.

It will be hours more before the last of the 7,800 official entrants, and maybe a couple of thousand more who ran anyway, finally come to the end of their exhausting journey.

The big names arrived to the cheering throngs what is now nearly two hours ago. Bill Rodgers was first. Actually, a cop on a motorcycle was first, but Bill Rodgers was right behind him with a record time of two hours, nine minutes, and twenty-seven seconds. It was his second straight Boston Marathon victory.

Appropriately, Bill Rodgers is from Boston and he sells sneakers. For accomplishing his feat, Bill Rodgers had a laurel wreath placed upon his head, and a medallion was hung around his neck by the governor of Massachusetts, Edward King. The crowd booed Edward King on Patriots Day in Boston.

What else the winner of the Boston Marathon gets is a bowl of beef stew. I hope they never change that. What occurred here Monday in cold and drizzling rain was a sporting event—a human event—that is still relatively pure and unspoiled by promoters and agents and television, not to mention candybar and beer companies that want to get their names in the newspapers.

Bill Rodgers crossing the finish line at the Boston Marathon Monday was as thrilling a moment as I have seen in sport. My goosepimples from the cold doubled in size.

But what is even more thrilling is watching now, watching the stragglers, the "nobodies"—the teachers, the housewives, the doctors, maybe even a cop or two, or Joe Futz the insurance salesman from Pottstown—push their tired and worn bodies to limits they probably never believed possible when they ended a two-pack-a-day habit and decided to become athletes.

Grown men are hugging each other at the finish line. Many are finishing in tears. A medical center is located in a nearby garage. Freezing, cramping runners are wrapped in cellophane sheets and placed on cots. Doctors move from cot to cot treating frightful blisters. It's the rescue center after an earthquake.

I asked a man who looked like he was dying was it worth it.

"I ran the sonuvabitch," he said, "and I beat it." On his soaked T-shirt were the words, "Human Power."

As I looked at him, I thought about Bob Horner of the Braves and Pete Rose and what's-his-name Parker with the Pirates and Reggie Jackson of the Yankees, as well as Jim Rice of the Red Sox, who at that moment was only a few blocks away at Fenway Park, lolling around in left field for something like $50,000 a game.

Columnist Leigh Montville of The *Boston Globe* was apparently thinking of the same sports millionaires' club when he so aptly advanced the Boston Marathon Monday morning.

"There are no agents involved today," he wrote. "There are no options being played out, no deals being made, no fleets of Mercedes being pulled into any special parking lot.

"The athlete of the day is an athlete, period, not some modern Clark Gable figure, some *Photoplay* sports god, cast in bubblegum and set atop some big rock-candy mountain.

"He is one of us again. As he runs the grand promenade from Hopkinton to the Prudential Center, he beckons us to come along, to sweat and enjoy. . . .

"The runner in the eighty-third Boston Marathon returns fun and games to fun and games. Somehow, he makes the rest of the sports page seem silly on this day."

You sense the trend vividly here, the fitness trend that has 20 million Americans running, the trend that has the rest of us at least thinking every time we light up a cigarette or spend another wasted, stinking afternoon watching overpaid balloonheads perform on that wretched talking box in our living rooms.

Grandmothers and grandfathers ran in the Boston Marathon Monday. A woman was telling her dinner companions in Boston Sunday night about announcing to her husband two years ago she was going to run in this race. His reply can't be printed here. But Monday, she showed him. There was a wheelchair brigade in the race. There were no fat people. A husband and wife, wearing matching outfits, finished together in an embrace.

Human Power. May the first promoter with the idea to turn this event into $100,000 Colgate Foot Race of Champions and move it to Las Vegas be shot at the next available sunrise, and may Howard Cosell never get close to it.

For the record, the Boston Marathon champion, Bill Rodgers, made a salary of $7,000 last year selling shoes. He drives a dented, 1963 Volkswagen. He lives with his wife, and they pay $165 a month in apartment rent.

Somebody once asked him what he thought of golf as a sport.

"You get about the same exercise in a hand of canasta," he said.

In the same interview, he was asked if he thought Joe Namath was a great athlete because he could throw a football straight.

"I'll be running over his grave," was Bill Rodgers' answer.

Farewell to Sports

I saw my first major league baseball game in Clark Griffith Stadium in Washington, D.C., in July of 1959. You don't forget your first major league baseball game.

The White Sox were visiting the Senators. Billy Pierce pitched for Chicago. Camilo Pascual pitched for Washington. It was a warm night.

There was no score until the top of the seventh. Nellie Fox, who is dead now, singled home two runs for the Sox. Jim Landis brought Fox home with a sacrifice fly. Chicago led, 3-0.

Pierce had a no-hitter into the eighth. Ron Samford broke it up with a double to left field that scored a runnêr who had walked. The final score was 3-1.

Harmon Killebrew struck out three times. Luis Aparicio made two great plays at shortstop. I drank three Cokes and ate two boxes of popcorn and one bag of peanuts. At one point during the game, I looked around at the stadium and spotted an enclosed seating area behind home plate. There were men inside.

"Who are those people?" I asked my adult companion.

"Sportswriters," he said.

"Do they see all the games?" I went on.

"It's their job," he said. "They don't even have to pay to get in."

That settled it. I was twelve. Anybody, I figured, could become a doctor or a lawyer or a car dealer. Nineteen years later, I don't own a boat, but I've seen a lot of ball games free. And once I went to Callaway Gardens for four days to cover a water-ski tournament and the newspaper paid for it. I made the right choice of professions.

A week from Sunday, I am moving my typewriter to another part of the building. My boss and I went through lengthy negotiations concerning the switch.

"Grizzard," he said, "Your column is moving out of sports."

"Okay," I said.

Both The *Constitution* and The *Journal* are taking on new graphic faces, and I am to be relocated in a new section that will concern itself with news of city and state. I am told I can still write about sports but that when I choose not to, I won't have to feel guilty about it anymore.

I'm not very good at goodbyes, but before I go, there's a few more things I wanted to say:

—— I will never get used to Al Ciraldo not broadcasting Georgia Tech basketball games and Whack Hyder not coaching the team.

—— The best place to watch a baseball game is Wrigley Field in Chicago. The worst place is Yankee Stadium because crazy people go there.

—— My favorite sportswriter is Dan Jenkins. My favorite sports book is *Semi-Tough*, which he wrote. My favorite sports movie is not *Semi-Tough*. It is *Bless the Beasts and the Children,* a movie about shooting buffalo.

—— Soccer and hockey are boring. Horse racing is exciting only if you have money on the race. The Indianapolis 500 should be against the law. Wrestling is fake. Organized sports are harmful to children under twelve. Tennessee has the most obnoxious fans in college football. Alabama is second. I'll be glad when Woody Hayes retires.

—— Jesse Outlar wrote the best line I ever read about the National Basketball Association's long-winded playoff system: "If the NBA had been in charge of World War II, Japan and Germany would still be in the running."

—— I still miss Harry Mehre.

—— The sixteenth hole at Augusta National on a Sunday in April is the prettiest place in the world.

—— There will never be another pitcher like Sandy Koufax, another college quarterback like Joe Namath, another stockcar driver like Fireball Roberts, another stockcar writer like Bill Robinson, another golfer like Arnold Palmer, and I wish Rod Laver were twenty years old.

—— I loved it when Dan Jenkins wrote, "The only thing worse than track is field."

—— Al McGuire is beautiful. Once he said, "The only time winning is important is in surgery and war."

—— The second best line I ever read about the NBA's long-winded playoff system came from a guy in Philadelphia who said, "The only uncomfortable thing that lasts longer than an NBA season is pregnancy."

—— Of all the people I have met in sports, Dan Magill, the Georgia tennis coach, is the most unforgettable. "Can I help you?" asks the waitress. "A Heineken's, honeykins," replies Magill, "and a sliced, barbecue, pork-pig sandwich."

—— If Alex Hawkins says that pot was planted in his car, I believe him.

• 6 •

FERGIT, HELL!

I make no apologies for anything that appears in this chapter. I was born in the South and I love the South and once my grandmother told me we had a relative who fought with Stonewall Jackson. That would be Uncle Beauregard Grizzard who died in 1882, singing "Dixie" and hating Yankees.

Homer Southwell, Author

Occasionally, Ludlow Porch of WRNG radio calls me on the telephone. That is because I knew him before he was a star. I knew him when he was a mild-mannered insurance claims adjuster with a secretary and a messy desk in Decatur. Ludlow wasn't as much fun in those days, but he caused less trouble.

What Ludlow Porch does for a living now is host two hours of madness on Atlanta's all-talk WRNG. Five days a week, he is set loose on the air to say anything he wants to. Listeners call in and the result is the city's most popular radio show.

You may recall Ludlow's revealing the "Montana Myth." There is no Montana, he said. Or the Great Parsley Debate. Ludlow claimed parsley causes several rare blood diseases and shortness of breath.

Recently, he set about to prove smoking is the cause of homosexuality. He also interviewed an official from HEW who announced all marriage licenses issued in the seven Southern states—"and parts of Florida"—since 1958 were void because they were issued outside HEW guidelines.

"The only exceptions," Ludlow explained, "are marriages conducted on navigable waterways or in a Winnebago."

Ludlow called last week to tell me about Homer Southwell.

Homer Southwell, it turns out, has been a frequent guest on the

Porch program. He is the alleged author of books assailing the constant flow of Northerners southward.

"First he wrote, *Yankee Go Home,*" Ludlow said, "and then followed it with a sequel, *And Stay There.* He is terribly disturbed about Yankees who come South because of our warm weather and good food."

Homer Southwell has stirred the masses. Calls come by the thousands when he is a Porch guest. Irate transplanted Northernpersons want him lynched. Southerners who share his feelings concerning Yankee emigration want his statue erected on the grounds of the state capitol. A Porch sponsor canceled.

I caught up with Homer Southwell Thursday as he worked away in his East Cobb County home.

"I'm starting my first novel," he said. "It's called *Return to Marietta* or *East of the Big Chicken.*"

The hero of his latest literary endeavor, Homer said, will be a fellow named Jimmy James Cheetwood.

"Jimmy James is a real person I knew growing up in Cobb County," Homer explained. "He was the meanest man I have ever seen. He was so mean, he was *born* with a tattoo. They think he inherited it from his mama."

I probed deeply into Homer Southwell's disdain for Northern infiltration into the South. After all, I pointed out, the war has been over 113 years.

"So what?" Homer asked. "They're flocking down here by the millions. What will happen to our wonderful Southern way of life if we let every fast-talking Yankee who wants to live on our precious soil?"

Homer immediately launched into a tirade. I hurriedly copied down all the remarks I could follow:

—— "I wouldn't go North for a three-week orgy with 'Charlie's Angels.' "

—— "I encourage ripping-off of Yankee tourists on the interstates. You don't even need a mechanic to do it. You just tell 'em you're going to change their shocks and then don't."

—— "The greatest form of birth control known to man is a Bronx accent."

—— "God lives somewhere in the Alpharetta area."

—— "I once made the mistake of dating a woman from Des Moines. She had hairy legs. All Yankee women have hairy legs."

Frankly, I had suspicions Homer Southwell might be a fraud, a figment of Ludlow Porch's weirdo imagination.

Then I asked him what he did for fun and relaxation when there is a break from the rigors of writing and Yankee-hating.

"I have a hobby I have enjoyed for years," Homer said. "Reading the *New York Times* obituary page."

Fergit, hell.

The Cyclorama: A Disgrace

The strains of "Dixie" come up softly at first and then grow louder and louder. Recorded musket fire bristles in the background. There is a vague human cry from somewhere in the distance. Perhaps it is a Rebel yell, or perhaps it is some mother's child catching a bullet 114 years ago.

"Ladies and gentlemen," booms a familiar voice, "this is Victor Jory."

I remember Victor Jory. Last time I saw him, he had a whip in his hand.

There are a couple of things that have always bothered me about the Battle of Atlanta production in Atlanta's Cyclorama:

The painting is from Milwaukee, and the man who does the narration, Victor Jory, played the part of a most hateful carpetbagger in *Gone with the Wind*. I don't forgive easily.

Today is Confederate Memorial Day. All state offices will be closed. The United Daughters will celebrate. I prepared by spending a morning revisiting the Cyclorama. It had been a few years.

The guns are still blazing out of Hurt House. Sherman still watches the "inferno" from his mounted perch. The Wisconsin farmer's eagle still soars above the battle. And there remains the classic portrait of brother meeting brother in the midst of hell.

One is dying. The other, his enemy, gives him water to ease the pain. "This," roars Victor Jory, "is not a memorial to the decay of brotherhood, but a memorial to the birth of freedom. . . ."

For a time Tuesday morning, I was alone with the *Battle of Atlanta*. Tourists weren't exactly tearing through the turnstiles.

I paid my two dollars. A young black woman took my ticket. She was polite and urged me to hurry. "The next presentation," she said, "is about to begin."

I noticed posters on the walls, posters asking donations for the Cyclorama. I walked up the winding staircase that leads to history in the round.

It took 8,000 pounds of paint to put the *Battle of Atlanta* on canvas. It has faded now. There are visible cracks.

Red is the dominant color around me. Victor Jory announces the earthen floor of the painting's three-dimensional foreground is "actual Georgia red clay." What did he expect?

Red covers the faces and chests of the dying and wounded figures that seem as real now as they did the first time a child looked upon them in amazement. ". . . Die they do by the thousands," says Victor Jory of a Confederate charge that was, perhaps, the South's last charge, on that day, July 22, 1864.

Once there was talk of moving the Cyclorama to another site. The building is old. It leaks. There was a fight for restoration funds, and somebody said, "If we don't do something soon, it will be too late."

It appears the Cyclorama will be restored now. Improvement can't come too soon.

Four ladies from someplace like Akron finally joined me and broke my solitude Tuesday morning. When the presentation was over, we walked outside. I heard one of the ladies say to the others, "From the looks of this place, the South has finally forgotten the war."

This shrine is, frankly, a disgrace. The years of neglect are taking their toll. And we really don't have "Dixie" to play anymore. "Dixie" is considered offensive.

One of the papers had to remind Atlanta readers that today is Confederate Memorial Day. Most of them wouldn't have known, otherwise. I heard a woman on a radio show the other day say, "We celebrate Confederate Memorial Day up North. We call it a tribute to Yankee marksmanship." That got a big laugh from a group of southerners.

I don't want to rally around the Rebel flag again. I don't have a picture of Stonewall Jackson over my fireplace.

I do know, however, Robert E. Lee once said of the men we are supposed to be honoring today, "They were asked to give more than should have been expected of them," and I know that they gave it.

That's good enough for me.

The Truth About General Lee

Dr. Emory Thomas came on the line from Athens where he is a professor of history at the University of Georgia.

My question was quick and to the point:

"Is it true," I asked, "what they are saying about Gen. Robert E. Lee?"

No true sons or daughters of the Confederacy have had a decent night's sleep since President Carter, of all people, visited Gettysburg the other day and said His Majesty General Lee made a "big mistake" in the key battle of the Civil War.

Heresy. Pure and simple.

To make matters worse, there is a new book concerning Lee, *The Marble Man*, in which a Nashville military historian named Thomas Connelley fires further salvos at Our Hero and Leader.

Lee, says Connelley, was a man obsessed with failure, who suffered from "repressed vibrance." ("He would have been a hell-raiser if he had had the opportunity" is Dr. Thomas' translation of that phrase.)

Connelley also says Lee was depressive because of an unhappy marriage to a woman prematurely arthritic and that he used religion as a crutch.

Dr. Thomas recently reviewed *The Marble Man* for *Virginia Magazine.*

"The reference to religion," he explained, "is basically that if Lee met anything he couldn't deal with or didn't want to deal with, he would simply put it off on Almighty Providence."

But that didn't answer my original question. Did, I asked Dr. Thomas—a Civil War authority and a native of Richmond, by-God Virginia—Robert E. Lee blow Gettysburg?

"Lee, himself, said it was all his fault," Dr. Thomas began, "and it was."

Allow the shock to wear off, and then we will continue. Recall that Lee had invaded the North in hopes of a major confrontation with the enemy. Although there was no clear-cut victor at Gettysburg, the loss of manpower and supplies Lee's Army of Northern Virginia suffered was the knockout blow of the war to the South.

I pressed for more details from Dr. Thomas as a tear rolled down my cheek.

"My interpretation," he went on, "is that Lee got up there, figured he had come all that way, and had gone to all that trouble and that it was maybe his last chance to do it big and do it right.

"He wanted a showdown battle. He had tried to turn the left and he had tried to turn the right. Finally, he said to hell with it, and went right up the middle.

"It was suicide."

Dr. Thomas does take some of the blame away from Lee. Ewell, he explained, didn't occupy Cemetery Ridge the first day he arrived, allowing the Yankees to take that strategic position.

Lee wanted Longstreet to take Little Roundtop. Longstreet could have, had he moved earlier.

"One of the problems," said Dr. Thomas, "was that the Army of Northern Virginia was basically a command of gentlemen. Lee didn't give his commanders specific orders. He just suggested what they *might* do."

Lee ordered a charge, said the professor, "at the geographic center of the entire Yankee army."

Get the picture: Flags are flying, bugles blowing, bands playing. And men dying. Fifteen thousand Confederate soldiers tried to take Cemetery Ridge from the Yankees. Maybee 300 made it to the top. They were easily repulsed.

"They were doomed," said Dr. Thomas, "before they started."

We talked more. About Pickett's tears after the battle. About his dislike for Lee after the war. About Lee making the same mistake in the Seven Days Battle. About Lee's words, "It is good that war is so terrible, else men would grow too fond of it."

My heart breaking, an idol from my first history class crushed to mortal dust, I had to ask one more question:

Would the South have been better off with somebody else in charge of its military besides Lee?

"The best answer for that," Dr. Thomas said, "is certainly it would. Then, it would have lost the war about two years earlier."

• 7 •

ON THE ROAD

My favorite place to be is home. I know all the bartenders and where to get great barbecue. But a man can have an occasional high time in Memphis, the music is good in Dallas, Washington isn't such a bad place if you don't have to work there, and they like to hear me talk in New York.

And once an angel cooked my breakfast in Tellico Plains, Tennessee. . . .

"Honk If You Love Elvis"

MEMPHIS — I don't know what I expected Wednesday at Graceland on the first anniversary of the death of Elvis Presley. Graceland is the walled mansion in Memphis where Elvis, the late King, lived and died and is buried behind the swimming pool, next to his mother.

I didn't expect dignity because neither Elvis' life nor his death was dignified. He lived in a world of glitter and rhinestones and $50,000 automobiles, and he died in his pajamas on his bathroom floor.

One doctor said death was from "acute blood pressure changes," caused by straining for a bowel movement.

But I expected at least a certain reverence. A certain respect for Elvis' memory. A man born to near-poverty rose to fame and the millions that went with it. And I have read so much about the love of his fans.

A sign on a car in downtown Memphis this week read, "Elvis— We Will Love You Forever." Another said, "Honk If You Love Elvis."

I expected respect and reverence at least. I found a circus. Worse, I found a carnival of money-changers.

It was hell-hot Wednesday morning, and the line in front of the wall at Graceland was long and barely moving. Thousands waited hours for a chance to file past the gravesite.

Across the street from the mansion were rows of Elvis souvenir shops. Hawkers were at every corner, and they worked the ready-to-buy crowd with the intensity of a worrisome fly. They had to be shooed away.

For sale: Elvis T-shirts, Elvis posters, Elvis plates, Elvis clocks, Elvis portraits, pictures of Elvis riding horses, pictures of Elvis riding motorcycles.

For sale: Elvis belt buckles, Elvis hats, Elvis bumper stickers, Elvis black armbands, and a game called "King of Rock 'n Roll," a sort of Elvis Presley monopoly board with play money, lots of it.

For sale: copies of Elvis' driver's license, copies of Elvis' birth certificate, copies of Elvis' high school report card (F's in English), copies of Elvis' marriage license, and for $5, get your picture taken sitting in Elvis' first Cadillac, a 1956 purple El Dorado.

For sale: Elvis Frisbees.

Flowers and a picture of a hound dog covered the Graceland lawn. Flowers covered the gravesite. A pink teddybear had been placed nearby. "I love you, Elvis," read a card around its neck. It was signed "Your teddybear, Columbus, Ohio."

Back at the gate, national guardsmen, in the city because of the police and firemen's strike, had stopped allowing people inside the gates.

"The family wants a little time to itself," said a burly sergeant.

In came Vester Presley, Elvis' uncle, blowing the horn of his Cadillac. His books are on sale at the gate. In came Ginger Alden, Presley's girlfriend who was with him at the time of his death. She rode in the back of a car with two men in the front.

Later she would be driven out again. She would be in the back seat, crying. Twenty people would rush to the window of the car to snap pictures of her. Look for those pictures on sale here next year.

A Memphis garbage truck pulled out of the Graceland driveway Wednesday after its daily pickup.

A man standing in the line said to his wife, "Grab a sack of that garbage, honey. No telling what it would sell for."

Texas Chic

DALLAS — There are a lot of things I like about Texas, but let me start at the top: in Texas, they sell barbecue downtown.

Take the lovely city of Dallas, for instance. A person can step right out of his hotel onto bustling Commerce Street, walk into Neiman-Marcus for a little shopping, and then lunch at Gus's or the Copper Cow or the Golden Steer and feast upon sliced barbecue sandwiches in a modern, urban setting of glass and steel and taxi and bus exhaust fumes.

You can't do that in most other cities.

There are good barbecue places accessible *from* Atlanta—like Harold's at the federal pen—but in mid-city, the closest thing to barbecue is a truckload of hogs in a traffic jam on the downtown connector.

Regardless of where barbecue is eaten, its flavor and enjoyment are always enhanced by something cold to drink—preferably beer.

In Texas, you can have Coors beer with your downtown barbecue. Coors, the Colorado light nectar, is the favorite beer of Americans who can't get it. Coors isn't sold in Atlanta. It is smuggled into the city by airline stewardesses who fly out West.

I was in Dallas over the weekend for the Texas-Oklahoma football game, a good excuse for three-fourths of the population of both states to get drunk for three days.

Before the game, I stepped out of my motel room onto bustling Commerce Street, walked into Neiman-Marcus for a little shopping, and then had lunch at the Golden Steer in a modern urban setting of glass and steel and taxi and bus exhaust fumes.

I ordered two sliced barbecue sandwiches and a Coors and settled into thinking about why Texas has suddenly become so popular and chic. Do you realize New York City has even discovered Texas?

One of the hottest spots in town is a country music bar where they serve the Texas state beer, Lone Star, in longneck bottles, and the clientele wears cowboy hats and boots and is attempting to learn the correct pronunciation of "sumbitch."

I asked a Texas native about the phenomenon.

"Texas just *feels* good," he said, and "it encompasses about everything. We're out West, but we're also down South. And look what we've done for the culture of this country."

The list of Texas' cultural donations is staggering. Texas gave us chicken-fried steak and Walter Cronkite. It gave us Dan Jenkins and his marvelous book, *Semi-Tough.*

Don Meredith is from Texas. So is Phyllis George, and I would imagine most of the Dallas Cowboys cheerleaders. Which brings up the musical question: Whatever happened to the Kilgore Junior College dancing rangerettes?

And you know who else is from Texas. Willie Nelson. His buddy, Waylon Jennings, says everybody in Austin thinks when they die, they go to Willie's house.

Dallas is my favorite big city in Texas.

"It's nothing more than a big Mineola," said another native. "Dallas is made up of all the people who left the farm and learned to count."

But the people are friendly in Dallas. A hotel clerk didn't ask me for a major credit card and actually said when I checked in, "Nice to have you with us."

And Dallas is the home of the annual State Fair of Texas, perhaps the last of the great expositions of its kind in America. It opened Saturday and it will run two weeks and attract over 3 million visitors.

There will be horse shows and a rodeo, and livestock exhibits and gospel and country singing. The carnival midway is massive. See the world's smallest woman for a quarter. She's only four inches tall. See Emmett, the Alligator Boy. Billy Earl and his wife, Clovis, come every year all the way from Lubbock.

"This is where we spent our honeymoon," Clovis smiled

proudly. Billy Earl looked embarrassed and disappeared to look at the tons of prime meat on the hoof down at the cattle barn.

Texans are a proud and courageous lot. Remember the Alamo. The University of Texas football team, incidentally, had about the same chance against Oklahoma Saturday at Dallas' Cotton Bowl. But they are a little crazy when it comes to football in Oklahoma, where the school president once said, "We want a university the football team can be proud of."

Texans simply know themselves, what they like, and what they expect of each other. I heard it put this way from across the bar after a few more Coors at the Golden Steer Saturday: "If you don't like Willie Nelson, longneck beers, long-legged women, rodeos, football, barbecue, the state fair, and an occasional fist fight, then you ain't no Texan. You just live here."

Cash Only

WASHINGTON — Here I sit in a big hotel room.

What fun.

When I was a kid, I liked hotel rooms because I could jump on the beds. Now, I like them because I can throw towels on the floor and somebody else will pick them up.

Washington is full of big hotels, because this is an important city and a lot of people from other places come here to work and to visit and to be politicians.

I suppose that the reason they always give you a booklet on security when you check into a Washington hotel is that there are lots of politicians here.

My booklet says, "Do not leave money, jewelry or other valuables in your room."

It also says, "Please bolt your door. This will shut out all keys. Also, insure that the security chain is engaged and that the connecting room door is locked."

Some rooms in Washington come with their own German shepherds. They are the ones nearest the Capitol.

This is a classy hotel I'm in. I knew it was classy when I saw the room service menu. The only thing cheaper than the $4.95 cheeseburger is a cup of coffee, which is $1.50.

One morning, I saw a fight between two taxicab drivers in the parking lot of my hotel. They were arguing about whose turn it was to pick up a fare. One driver bopped the other driver in the face, thus settling the argument. The other driver threw a rock at his colleague's cab as it sped away with the fare. Like I said, this is a classy hotel.

Hotel front desks are usually manned and womanned by young people who are very clean, wear expensive clothes and have a habit of acting snooty. Whatever happened to the friendly night clerk in his undershirt reading tomorrow's race entries?

Even the bellmen have come up in the world in today's hotels. The bellmen here wear red uniforms like the one Omar Sharif wore when he danced with Julie Christie at the Leningrad ball.

There is one staggering problem in hotels today, however. Hotels do not like to deal in cash. They abhor cash, as a matter of fact, along with anybody who would deface their front desk with it.

I deal in cash. Credit cards are financial heroin.

"May I see a credit card?" the snooty young woman at the front desk asked me when I arrived at my Washington hotel.

"Don't carry them," I said.

She called over the assistant manager.

"He doesn't carry credit cards," she said to him.

A lady behind me gasped in horror.

The assistant manager called over the manager.

"He doesn't carry credit cards," the manager was told.

I rattled my change as loudly as possible.

"If you don't have a credit card, sir" the manager asked me, his hands squarely on the hips of his designer trousers, "then how do you propose to pay your bill?"

Now, he had me.

"Cash," I said. "American," I quickly added, hoping to regain at least some face.

They wanted to see it.

A half hour passed before a decision was made. Finally, after I paid in advance, I was allowed to proceed to my room. They gave me a little card to read on the way up, however.

It said, "Because you have made a cash payment and did not present a major credit card at the time of your arrival, our operational procedure is to request that you make all further payments in restaurants, bars, and gift shop at the time the bills are presented."

How can you trust a man who carries cash?

The only time cash is accepted cheerfully in a hotel is when you give it to a bellman in the form of a tip.

After the experience of checking in, I followed a squatty version of Omar Sharif at the Leningrad ball up to my room.

He put up my bags, switched on the lights and the air-conditioner, and then waited impatiently by the door for his tip.

"Got change for a hundred?" I asked.

"No," he answered, "but I can get it from the front desk. I heard some yahoo just checked in using cash."

We both got a big laugh over that.

Disco Zoo

NEW YORK — The hottest spot in town is Studio 54, a disco on West 54th Street, appropriately enough. Not just anybody can get into Studio 54.

Here is how it works: every evening at midnight, a throng gathers outside and waits to be chosen for entrance. The lucky ones are then allowed to pay $20 per couple for admission. Once inside, there is a huge dance floor, flashing lights, and music to give birth to a buffalo by.

The dancing and the music and the lights go nonstop until dawn, when many of the customers must scurry back to the sewers. These are the beautiful people? A regular had mentioned to me earlier, "Go stand by the men's room. You might seen Andy Warhol."

I'm not certain by what criteria entrants are selected. Judging from some of the clientele I saw, it would appear to be in your favor to come from another planet. Besides the men's and ladies' rooms, there is one marked "it."

I was given some advice on getting inside: "Make sure you dress in something unusual, or grease the doorman with a fifty."

I needed the fifty for breakfast the next morning. I wore my college rush outfit—a navy blazer, gray slacks, yellow Polo tie and Weejuns.

I was inside in a New York second.

"Funky outfit," said the doorman. To him, a wetsuit tux and snow shoes are normal.

"Disco" is our nation's latest nervous breakdown. Studio 54 is the home office. Truman Capote might drop by with Norman Mailer. For that matter, Godzilla might shake his booty with Yasser Arafat while Leon Spinks plays the flute. This is a strange place.

There was a movie made about disco, *Saturday Night Fever*. In the movie, they danced the hustle, and the moves were graceful and with style.

In Studio 54, they dance something that resembles a monkey halfway there on an LSD trip. Say it ain't so, John Revolta.

I paid my admission and went directly to the men's room to interview Andy Warhol. He wasn't there. Fan Man was. Fan Man wore a ribbon in his hair, lipstick, a long skirt and peered out from behind a fan.

"Funky outfit," he said as I walked past him.

There was more. Golden Boy strolled through. He was a stunning blond. For the evening, he had chosen a sleeveless blouse, open to the navel. He carried a gold purse and wore a gold lamé skirt and gold bedroom slippers from the Aladdin collection.

Later, he danced with Peter Punk. Peter Punk came in his father's old bowling shirt, which he wore outside his mother's jodphurs. He had a black ring painted around his left eye.

There was a girl in fatigues carrying a hula hoop. There was another girl in a wraparound evening dress she had fashioned from a bedsheet. She had washed her hair in Thousand Island dressing and blown it dry with an acetylene torch. Fan Man was looking better all the time.

My companion and I eventually braved the dance floor. We immediately provoked stares. My companion was a girl person in a chiffon, ankle-length dress, appropriate for dinner at "21."

"Funky outfit," said the girl in the bedsheet dancing with Hoola-Hoop Hattie next to us.

Studio 54 is loud and kinky and, on this night at least, predominantly gay. Teenage boys wait tables in silver underpants, tennis shoes and nothing else. After they clean your table, they dance on it.

Two models show up in running shorts, pull off their blouses and dance barebreasted. Shirtless men dance with other shirtless men. I puffed a Marlboro. Most of the crowd rolled their own.

In the wee hours, it was time to leave. There was still the mob scene outside. As I walked through the crowd, a breathless girl grabbed my arm.

"How did you get in?" she asked, in full swoon.

With an air of self-assurance, I replied, "My funky outfit," and disappeared down the street into a fog of reality.

"Chicken" and the "Worm"

PLAINS — A regular walked into Billy Carter's Service Station one hot afternoon last week and greeted Leon, the man who takes up money for gas and beer.

"Last time I saw you," he said, "We were both drunk."

"Believe we were," agreed Leon.

"We go in them bad places, don't we?" the man continued.

"Them dives," said Leon.

"Them places we go in," the man went on, "are so bad they got blood on the ceiling. Place with blood on the floor don't worry me. Place with blood on the ceiling, that's a tough place."

He noticed a jar on the side of the bar. The jar had money inside it.

"What's that for?" he asked Leon.

"For 'Chicken'," Leon replied. "We're gonna get him in the state senate. You gonna help us?"

"Damn right," said the man. "I'd do anything to get rid of that damn Hugh Carter."

Some introductions are probably necessary. The Hugh Carter here is Cousin Hugh Carter Sr., antique dealer, state senator, worm grower and author of the book *Cousin Beedie and Cousin Hot,* in which he wrote all sorts of things about First Cousin Jimmy and First Cousin Billy and anybody else who came to mind.

Hugh Carter Sr. lives in Plains, and he is running for re-election as state senator from the Fourteenth District. The primary approaches on August 8th.

"Chicken" is another story. He is Malcolm "Chicken" Wishard, a local farmer with no political experience to speak of. He's the man the regulars at Billy Carter's Service Station want to see whip the pants off Hugh Carter in the election.

That includes Billy himself.

"Miss Lillian's with us, too," said Leon. "She said she would spend every dime she had to see Chicken whip that damn Hugh Carter. Billy's done give his dime."

It took some talking and a six-pack, but I finally got to the bottom of this split in the Carter political camp. For one thing, Hugh's book didn't set well with the family. And for another, said a woman at Billy's, "there never has been no love lost between Billy and Hugh, and Miss Lillian and Billy are just alike."

Chicken Wishard's campaign was cranking up full blast at Billy's this afternoon. Leon passed out cards that read, "Help Chicken Take the Worm."

The "Worm" reference is to Hugh Carter, of course, the self-styled "Nation's Worm King." Even Mrs. Chicken dropped by for a visit.

"Why do they call Chicken 'Chicken'?" she was asked.

"When he was a little boy," she answered, "he was the first one in the family to get chickenpox."

Leon calls him "One-Eyed Chicken."

"That's because he ain't got but one good eye," said Leon. Leon also had a stack of campaign posters with Chicken's smiling face. Somebody put an empty beer can on the stack of posters.

"Get that off of there," Leon screamed. "You might get beer in Chicken's good eye."

I pressed for more details on campaign issues.

"Only issue I know," said Leon, "is we can't stand Hugh Carter and we finally got somebody to run against him. You can talk to Chicken. He's loud and if he walked in here right now, you'd think he was half a fool. But he ain't. He's a good man."

Billy Carter would eventually drop by the station. He was sipping something clear over ice. The tourists flocked around him. He signed autographs, posed for pictures, and sold six-packs of Billy Beer for $2.60. The local line is, "Jimmy's making $200,000 a year running the country, and Billy's already made $500,000 running his mouth."

And Billy would do his best for Chicken too.

"We need two things from you to help Chicken," he said to a farmer who came in for refreshment.

"What's that?" asked the farmer.

"Your vote and your money," said Billy.

I had to ask Billy Carter how he could go against his own flesh and blood. "Isn't this man your cousin?" I said.

"He ain't my cousin," Billy answers. "I gave him away."

Riding the High Lonesome

ON A GEORGIA BACKROAD — There are only two sounds out here. Four tires are humming as they hug the taxpayers' asphalt on Georgia 15. And the radio—God bless an automobile radio—has me in touch with you wouldn't believe the faraway places.

I am constantly turning the dial. Voices with no faces fade in and voices with no faces fade out. But at least there are voices, and without them the loneliness would creep even closer.

I have just departed from Sandersville, northbound through the deep-hole blackness the night brings to middle-eastern Georgia. There was a shooting in Louisville, clear-channel WHAS reports, but invading static keeps me from the details.

Dallas comes in loud and clear. It will be nice in Dallas tomorrow, with highs in the mid-seventies. I even pick up Cleveland.

You know they tried to recall the mayor in Cleveland. Now, the city council has been charged with accepting kickbacks. Things are tough all over.

Chicago's country WMAQ, an old friend, is beaming to thirty-eight states and Canada. A man sings a song that includes the line, "Plant them 'taters, and pull up another tomorrow."

It is difficult to avoid a hockey game, turning the dial on late-night radio. Hockey is enough of a problem for me in person. On the radio, it might as well be the noon news from Mars.

"Ro-jay brings the puck to center ice! Marcham-bo checks him there. Jablare intercepts, and there is a whistle for icing the puck!"

I am on the fringes of Hancock County, Georgia, listening to a man from Fort Wayne, Indiana, describe the actions of twelve foreigners on ice skates, chasing a rubber disc.

I turn back to Cleveland.

My headlights tunnel through the darkness. The tall pines frame the road, and two beady pearls of light suddenly appear in the distance.

This is the Halloween season, but a stray dog crossing the road has simply turned its head toward the lights of the car, and its eyes have reflected back.

Give me a dime for every stray dog on every Georgia back road, and my creditors can relax. I'll take a quarter for every dead possum.

I am trying to make Atlanta and home before sleep takes me over. Interstate 20 is somewhere ahead, just out of a place called Siloam in Greene County. The interstate is an auto jet-stream after crawling over two-lane. There is no other traffic because of the late hour and because country people have been in bed for hours. They get up early out here, you know. Don't let the sun catch you a-restin'.

There are tiny frame houses here and there, but not a sign of life to go with them. I grew up in a frame house that went dark at an early hour. The peace and comfort it held until morning has been difficult to relocate.

Downtown Sparta approaches. There are street lights, but no people. The old tavern in the middle of town, a historic landmark, looks haunted. It probably is.

Sparta lasts thirty seconds. The village of White Plains will be next. I cross Copeland Creek and Whitter Creek. There is a newscast coming in from WCAU, Philadelphia. Damn, I'm a long ways from Philadelphia.

What I am thinking is maybe everybody ought to do this occasionally. I am at least free with my thoughts here. Out like this, a man can talk to himself and it seems perfectly natural. You can ask yourself a question on a Georgia back road and get an honest answer.

Finally, Siloam. Siloam won't awaken for hours yet. The interstate approaches, laden with eighteen-wheeled monsters with big eyes and loaded backs bound for the city.

Parting with Georgia 15 is more difficult than I figured it would be. I will be home in just over an hour, but I realize that out on that primitive stretch I had maybe stumbled upon one of the modern urbanite's last escapes. I had ridden about all that remains of the High Lonesome on a pony with automatic transmission.

Cleveland has faded off the radio. I turn the dial again and a preacher is chasing the devil out of Tulsa. "Be saved or be damned!" is his warning.

Rolling along the interstate, I search for another hockey game.

Covering the Arrival of Spring

HILTON HEAD ISLAND, S.C. — Soft rain is falling, the wind is blowing, and the skies are cloudy. But the temperature is pleasantly mild, and for three days previous to this one, late winter's coastal sun has shown brilliantly. I will be leaving here soon, and that thought saddens me.

I will miss my duck. There has never been such a duck. I don't know much about ducks, but this one lives in a lagoon outside my bedroom window and makes a sound like, "Braaaack! Braaaack!"

He works the night shift. His job is keeping the alligators awake. Ditto for any other creature within the sound of his quack.

He begins precisely at sundown. He doesn't hush until the dawn. I have nicknamed him "Hosea."

News from the outside world filters in slowly to a place like this. A big story here is that a cosmetic surgeon is moving to the island from Florida to take the wrinkles out for the summer parties at the Sea Pines Club.

That announcement brought an interesting remark in a local paper from a man identified as an "island punster."

"Instead of having your face lifted," he asked, "why not have your body lowered?"

So the Reggie Eaves controversy rages on back in Atlanta, does it? Here, they are more concerned about the bleak outlook for shrimp. No white shrimp have been seen in coastal waters for five weeks. The cost of appetizers goes up and up.

Coal strike? What coal strike? Bless my Lincoln Continental, the cost of a membership to the Sea Pines Club will go up from $3,000 to $5,000 come April 1.

There has been some interest, however, in the story out of Arkansas where the preacher put his deceased eighty-year-old mother in a freezer locker and then tried to raise her from the dead. The older retirees here are keeping a close eye on his progress.

I came here to cover the arrival of spring. It comes two weeks earlier to coastal paradise.

I lived without any spring at all for a couple of years. There are only two seasons in Chicago. Winter and the Fourth of July. A year ago today, I was in snow navel-high to a tall Yankee.

Missing springtime is like missing a woman. You never really noticed her and then she was gone, and all that she was returns and makes the separation even more painful.

I think I read this somewhere: "Springtime is the land awakening. The March winds are the morning yawn."

People are already on bicycle jaunts around the island here. Sunbathers were on the beach at Turtle Cove over the weekend. Two couldn't wait and hit the surf in mid-seventies temperatures.

Squirrels cavort everywhere. I saw a bluebird and a starling. Four deer crossed a road in the Sea Pines Plantation and loped casually through front yards of island residents.

Soon will come another sign of the season. I usually gauge the appearance of spring by the arrival south of the professional golf tournaments. Hilton Head's annual Heritage Classic, a prelude to Augusta National's Masters, is only a week away.

"The boats are already coming in," said a man in Harbor Town Tuesday. "The Heritage and spring brings them south."

Let It Be is docked from Ithaca. *Taranak* is here from Plymouth, Maine. *Ravissant* came down from Wilmington, Delaware. I see them and think of the old line about nobody ever retiring north.

The rain has stopped. There is a mist hanging over the marsh behind the Harbor Town Links' sixteenth green. The wind has ceased, and the stillness that has followed offers an added comfort.

Let them fight it out at City Hall, and where on earth is South Molucca, anyway? Spring is rushing in, and me and my duck wish you were here.

New York Subways

NEW YORK — I had planned to ride a lot of commuter trains around New York to practice for when Atlanta's new rapid rail system opens. That will be just as soon as the excavation is completed and the city is put back together again.

Presently, Atlanta looks like what Sherman would have left if he had been carrying bulldozers and jackhammers.

Also, I figured the subway would be the best means of transportation around New York, following the big snowstorm last week. After the snow came warmer temperatures and rain. The snow melted and the streets flooded.

The crud that normally just sits on the streets of New York started floating. Egg shells, potato peelings and salami sandwich parts I stepped over on 52nd Street passed by me again as I tried to cross 63rd.

I decided, however, to brave the flooded streets and to look for nonexistent empty taxicabs rather than attempt to take subway trains. That is beccause the snow and flooding were causing problems underneath New York, too.

One train on its way to New Jersey quit running in what they call a PATH tube somewhere underneath the Hudson River, speaking of floating crud. The people inside the train were three hours getting out.

"Everybody stayed calm," said one of the passengers. "We sang songs to pass the time."

If I were on a stranded commuter train on the way to New Jersey in a tube somewhere underneath the Hudson River, I would not stay calm, nor would I sing songs. That is because I can't panic and sing at the same time.

I heard some other horror stories about subway trains from native New Yorkers who ride them all the time.

"We were going along one morning," a young woman told me, "and it became quite obvious the train was going faster than it should have been. Everybody got a little nervous.

"Suddenly, the motorman walked out of his little compartment and threw up. He was drunk. At the next stop, they came and took him away."

Another commuter topped that.

"You never know what you'll see," he said, "I was on my way to

Queens. A guy and his wife or girlfriend got on the train having a big argument.

"They argue for four or five stops. They get louder and louder. Finally, the guy takes all he can stand and starts choking the woman. He chokes her until she's blue.

"Another man nearby grabs him and pulls him away from the woman and belts him one to settle him down. Soon as that happens, the woman cranks up and bops the poor guy who saved her life on the head with her pocketbook. He's out cold.

"At the next stop, the couple gets off and walks away arm-in-arm."

You simply have to know certain rules about riding commuter trains. Here are some I picked up in New York for Atlantans to remember in the future:

—— If somebody decides to choke his lover on a commuter train, don't interfere unless you want your head bashed in.

—— No matter how crowded a car looks, it will always hold one more.

—— Let sleeping drunks lie. Unless one happens to be driving your train. In that case, launch an immediate search of the cars for a priest.

—— In case of an emergency, like having to walk out of a tunnel, avoid the third rail. Ignore this rule and that sizzling sound is you, Bacon Face.

—— Discourage pickpockets and thieves. Swallow your wallet before entering the train.

—— If several young men in black leather jackets appear and ask for your wallet, do not tell them you swallowed it. Notice the fellow passenger who did is now minus one wallet and bleeding to death.

—— Never shove a friend off a platform in front of a speeding commuter train as a practical joke. Unless he gave you a hot foot when you were packed in like sardines during rush hour the day before. Then it's OK. You owe him one.

—— If you are now frightened about riding Atlanta's new commuter trains after reading all of the above, don't be. Remember, none of that could ever happen in our city.

Saltines and Solzhenitsyn

TELLICO PLAINS, TENN. — I had been days without a newspaper, locked away in a careless world of mountains, rivers, dirt roads, and a supply of Vienna sausage and sardines and a gift for which we can never offer enough gratitude: the saltine cracker.

God bless the saltine cracker, for it is constantly loyal in its service to enhance the flavor of even the barest edible. You could eat dirt with a packet of saltine crackers on the side.

I can't go many days without a newspaper because I can't go many days without certain information necessary to my peace of mind.

I need to make sure the world hasn't been blown away, and I need to keep up with the Dodgers. In this rustic village, which is located at the foot of some mountains near the Tennessee-North Carolina border, I purchased a newspaper and found the world still in one piece, which is more than I could say for the Dodgers.

Interest in the Dodgers is a carryover from my youth, but must a man have to explain every quirk of his character? The Dodgers, I read, have sunk to a lowly third. And the Giants, whom I hate, are still holding to first place. So help me Junior Gilliam, my favorite all-time Dodger, that can't last.

My companion and I needed a hot breakfast, if for no other reason than to take a brief leave from the joys of saltines. We walked into a place in Tellico Plains that was a combination beer joint and restaurant, mostly beer joint. The regulars were already at their stations. A card game of some variety was in progress, and an old man in a hat played the game with a boy-child on his knee.

"You have grits?" I asked the lady.

"No grits," she said. She was missing some teeth. "I could fix you potatoes."

Where does it say an angel must have teeth?

Over eggs and country ham and fried potatoes—the kind that are round and thin—I read the rest of the newspaper. Carter this. Carter that. All hail Proposition 13. And a bearded man had made a speech in the Harvard Yard and had said some nasty things about our country. He made the speech in his native tongue, Russian.

The man, who has never been to Tellico Plains, Tennessee, said we ought to eat dirt for awhile because we have become fat and too interested in material goods, like nice places to live and motorboats. He said we are suffering from a "moral poverty."

He said if he could change his country, which would put him in jail if he went back to it, he wouldn't use our country as a model.

I finished my breakfast and the newspaper, left a nice tip for the lady and walked out on the streets of Tellico Plains.

It was a gorgeous late spring day. Just beyond the fruited plain that surrounds the village was a mountain majesty more green than purple, but stunning nevertheless.

Passing by me were simple folk, dedicated to the day's work and the simple pleasures. Most of them, I am sure, had never heard of the Harvard Yard, much less of the bearded, exiled Russian author who spoke there.

A pickup truck passed through town, its rear bumper bearing a message I don't entirely agree with, but one I needed at the moment. The Dodgers were going badly and what the Russian had said upset me.

"America," read the sticker, "love it or leave it."

But where would you go, Mr. Solzhenitsyn? Where would you go?

• 8 •

RAILROAD BLUES

One day there won't be anymore trains to ride, and a part of me will die. The part that enjoys good conversation in the club car, morning coffee crossing the Potomac into Washington in the dining car, and little boys and old men who, as long as there are passenger trains, will stand beside the tracks and wave at them.

She Goes Bump in the Night

ABOARD THE FLORIDIAN — She used to have a more romantic name. She was The South Wind, and Johnny Cash mentioned her in a song: "She left me on The South Wind. . . ." When she was younger, she dazzled them with her speed and grace for over 2,000 miles of railed opulence.

Now, she is a tattered, financial mess that is unloved and unwanted. By way of introduction she is Amtrak's Chicago-to-Miami Floridian. She is old, she is slow, and she goes bump in the night.

The Floridian, nine cars and a brightly painted engine with a red snub-nose, left Miami just after dawn the morning before. The feminine personification is hardly applicable anymore. "It" passed through Fort Lauderdale and Orlando and rolled into Jacksonville nearly eight hours later.

Then, there was a westward swing through the flatlands of south Georgia, through Waycross, Valdosta and Thomasville, before a turn north into Alabama and Dothan, Montgomery and Birmingham.

The Floridian is notorious for running behind schedule. It is supposed to make the 2,576-mile journey between Chicago and Miami in just over thirty-seven hours, two full days and one night.

It is due in Birmingham's old Louisville and Nashville railroad

station—located in the middle of downtown—at 1:48 A.M. The rest
of Birmingham sleeps unaware in a soft rain.

A station agent, a baggage clerk and four passengers await the
train on a platform outside the station. Precisely at its expected
time of arrival, the Floridian's headlight peers around a corner
south of the station. "Train comin'," says the station agent. Train
comin' right on time, for a change.

I have made this trip before—Birmingham to Chicago, Chicago
to Birmingham—aboard The Floridian. Nashville and Louisville
are two of the stops in between. Rail travel remains a personal
adventure, despite the hardships it often entails. Although Amtrak, the government-subsidized authority that runs most of the
nation's remaining passenger trains, has managed to upgrade some
of its service, much of it remains a frayed relic of the past. The
Floridian falls into that category.

This train is one of Amtrak's biggest losers. This train, to borrow
from songwriter Steve Goodman, "got them disappearin' railroad
blues." This train is bound for a permanent siding if a providential
solution isn't found that would increase its ridership and cut down
its annual losses. The yearly deficit runs into millions.

One problem is its patronage is seasonal. "We are packed in the
summer," the dining car steward will tell me during the trip.
"We'll get two or three hundred people—most of them on vacation
to Florida—every day. After school starts back, that changes."

When the Floridian arrives in Louisville the next day at noon,
there will be twenty-one passengers on board.

A route change was one of the possible solutions Amtrak was
looking into before its management recommended complete scrap-
ping of the train. One proposal would have sent the Floridian
south out of Nashville into Atlanta, then to Macon and Savannah
—or to Macon, Albany, and Jacksonville. Public hearings were
held in Atlanta and in cities on the Floridian's route.

If Amtrak's board of directors goes along with management, Atlanta will remain the nation's largest city not receiving Amtrak
service. Southern Railway, which is not an Amtrak member, oper-
ates its own passenger train, the Southern Crescent, daily between

Atlanta and Washington, D.C., and three times a week between Atlanta, Birmingham, and New Orleans.

It is 713 rail miles between Birmingham and Chicago. Arrival in Chicago is scheduled at 9:02 P.M., nineteen hours after the Birmingham departure.

I am asleep thirty minutes out of Birmingham, despite a ride reminiscent of the tilt-a-whirl from county fairs past. For $71.50, I have purchased a first-class, one-way ticket that entitles me to a roomette accommodation—a private room with a bed that folds out of the wall. There is also a tiny toilet, a tiny lavatory, and a tiny closet inside.

A regular ticket—you sleep in a reclining seat in one of the day coaches—costs $35.00. Amtrak offers a number of special fares on the Floridian, including a Florida package that provides free use of a rental car for a week.

I can sleep on a train. Most people can't. I talked with a companion from the sleeper the next morning at breakfast.

"Sleep well?" I asked.

"No." he replied. "There are only three ways to go to sleep on this train. Be dead tired, dead drunk, or just plain dead."

The equipment was old when Harry and Bess were in the White House. It is vintage thirties and forties. It includes a baggage car, one Pullman, four day coaches, a diner, a rounded-end observation lounge car and a mail car tagging along at the end.

One of the coaches has a domed top with huge windows for sightseeing. It is located behind the diner. The greasy smoke from the diner's kitchen exhaust has opaqued the windows in the sightseeing dome car. The view from the back of the rounded-end observation lounge care is the front of the mail car. Nobody has ever accused Amtrak of planning ahead.

Two middle-aged women boarded the train in Louisville. They will go to Chicago, spend the night, and board another train the following evening for California. They will arrive almost three days later.

"The train is the only way to fly," one tells me.

"It's the ONLY way I'll fly," laughs her companion.

They are sitting in the lounge car, drinking beer. They have at least six beers each between Louisville and Chicago. When we reach Chicago, they are flying higher than anybody else on the train.

Out of Birmingham, the Floridian crosses Sand Mountain. There are two tunnels. It gradually rolls down into the Tennessee Valley and into Decatur, Alabama, where it crosses huge Wheeler Lake, a TVA reservoir. Dawn catches up just outside Nashville.

The terrain is hilly, the scenery is autumn-in-the-country. We are in Nashville's crumbling Union Station at 7 A.M. We cross the Cumberland River and travel on into the Kentucky morning. There is a quick stop in Bowling Green and then another river, the Barren. A brochure describing the Floridian's route says that near the Barren River is Lost River Cave, once the reputed hideout of the James Gang. The James Gang used to rob a lot of trains.

Out of Louisville, we cross the Ohio River after a forty-five minute wait for our turn on the bridge. "This is what kills us," says the dining car steward. "If it's between a freight and us, we always have to wait for the freight to pass first."

Across the river is Indiana. Indiana, I notice, is mostly small towns, with miles of pig farms, cow farms and horse farms and acres of dying corn stalks in between.

I also notice it is difficult for most people not to wave at a train when it passes by them. As long as there are passenger trains, there will be old men and little boys to wave at them.

At Bedford, Indiana, we stop for the southbound Floridian to pass. It is nearly empty, too.

My sleeping car porter is classic in the railroad sense. He is black, with a full crop of gray hair. He is smart in his black trousers and starched white frock. He is polite, patient and helpful. We talked about this train.

"I told 'em they ought to put this train through Atlanta five years ago." he says. "They ought to run it like the old Dixie Flyer that went to Atlanta and Albany and Jacksonville out of Chicago.

"That was some kind of a train. It left Jacksonville at night and got to Atlanta the next morning. The businessmen used to ride it.

A lot of people down there might ride it up to Atlanta now if Atlanta had any ball teams that were any good. But I don't believe Atlanta will ever have any ball teams that are any good. Do you?"

I said we would probably see pigs fly first.

The young man introduced himself as a songwriter from Nashville. He said the work was indoors and there was no heavy lifting, but he was having a hard time feeding himself.

"All day," he began, "I've been sitting here trying to write a good song about trains. 'City of New Orleans' really ran trains down. I just can't think of anything good to say."

The Floridian has been called the "dirtiest and smelliest" train on the Amtrak fleet. It isn't dirty. The smell is from another coat of fresh paint. The train is simply worn out and tired from overuse.

The cars were taken from the pool of equipment donated by the nation's freight-minded railroads when Amtrak was established in 1971. Some of the shorter runs are now using modern equipment built for Amtrak. The Floridian gets mostly scraps.

The Amtrak color scheme inside is a horrid scarlet and purple. The lounge car decoration is something from topless-a-go-go. It is kept spotless, however, by a pleasant bartender. Drinks are $1.50. Beer is 80 cents. The sterling of years past is gone from the dining car, but on each table sits a pair of fresh carnations.

The rest rooms are usable. In each are two signs. One is the familiar, "Kindly flush after each use EXCEPT when train is standing in the station." The other is, "It is impossible to clean rest rooms after every use. Please consider the next passenger."

It has been my experience that people who do not consider the next passenger—or people who can't read—are usually responsible for dirty rest rooms on trains.

The Floridian has had a number of accidents, although none has resulted in a passenger fatality. Once I was on this train and the bartender, a woman, passed around color photographs of a recent wreck. It was an unsettling experience.

A couple of months ago near Plant City, Florida, the Floridian hit a camper as the camper attempted to cross the tracks. Ten people in the camper died.

Some of the waiters were talking about train wrecks at lunch.

"My wife told me to get off this train," says one. "She say it's always trying to jump off into the woods."

"It's better than being on one of those big planes when it goes down," interrupts another. Everybody agrees to that.

One of the waiters was on the train when it hit the camper. He gives all the details. It is a gruesome description.

"Everybody is always wantin' to beat the train across the tracks," he says. "All they got to do is be patient for a couple of minutes and then go on about their business. Those people in the camper got plenty of time now," he goes on. "All the time they need."

Food is not included in the price of a ticket. A breakfast example is juice, two eggs, bacon or sausage, and coffee for $2.75. Lunch is a cheeseburger and potato chips for $2.35. Or an Amtrak Chef's Salad Bowl for $3.

Dinner might be a ten-ounce sirloin for $7.50. Or red snapper filet for $4.25. Or broiled chicken for $4.25. Wine is $2 per half-bottle.

The food is only fair. But the service is excellent. A conductor told me about the food on the old South Wind.

"The railroad raised its own pork," he said. "And everybody knew it had the best country ham anywhere. Everything was cooked right on the train. First thing the cooks would do is start baking. They baked all their own pies.

"Breakfast was something. Country ham, red-eye gravy on the grits, and hot biscuits. People would ride that train just to have the breakfast."

Grits aren't listed on the Floridian's menu. You have to ask for them. They are instant grits.

Smoking is not permitted in any of the coaches or in the dining car. You can smoke in the rest rooms, in private rooms, or in the lounge car. If you do not smoke, you will appreciate all that on a long train ride. If you do, it will drive you slightly crazy.

We arrive in Bloomington, Indiana, 200 miles out of Chicago, on time. Same for Lafayette, where the train station is the Lahr

Hotel in the middle of town. There are two hours to go. The route has straightened. It is smoother than before, which is saying very little. At times, we have crept along. After Lafayette, the train picks up speeds that reach eighty miles per hour. Just before sundown, I looked out the window near Cloverdale, Indiana, and saw three deer huddled together in a clearing in the woods.

Chicago comes at us suddenly. The lights of the Hancock Building and the Sears Tower are visible for miles over what is now flat terrain. At seven minutes until nine—nine minutes early—we are standing in Chicago's massive Union Station. A miracle has occurred.

I can't recommend the ride, but I can't curse it, either. There were no telephone calls. There was time to read, and time to think. A man who made the entire trip from Miami said he felt "defloovicated." I suppose that meant drained from the experience.

There was another conductor on the trip. His name was Mc-Whirter. He had been on this run for twenty-five years. Promotion, he felt, would have been the Floridian's saviour.

"There is nothing wrong with this train some advertising couldn't change," he began. "I pick up the paper everyday and see these big advertisements on airplanes. I never see anything on Amtrak.

"Why don't they spend a million dollars advertising this train? It would get 'em 5 million back. Nobody knows about us."

As he talked, I remembered a conversation with a Birmingham bartender long before Amtrak's management decided the Floridian should be scuttled. I asked him if people in Birmingham were concerned they might lose their train to Atlanta.

"What train?" he asked back.

Jimmy Harmon

It wasn't that long ago all little boys loved trains. Most of them grew out of it. Some of us didn't.

Jimmy Harmon, who was thirty-one, didn't. He knew the joy of dinner in the diner and watching America go by at eye level.

He knew about the lights of Washington passing behind the Southern Crescent as it pulls away from Union Station on its daily run to Atlanta. He knew about crossing the Potomac and catching pitch darkness in the woodlands of northern Virginia, rolling gently on Southern rails.

And morning on the Southern Crescent, he knew about that. Breakfast at sunrise in the mountains near Toccoa. Then, Gainesville, and finally Atlanta.

Atlanta is bustling and traffic-snarled as the train arrives here shortly before 9 o'clock. And Atlanta in her morning greenery from the window of a train can be a magnificent way to welcome another day.

Just a few days ago, Jimmy Harmon experienced all that again. He rode the train from Atlanta to Washington and from Washington back through Atlanta and on to New Orleans—the Southern Crescent from start to finish.

It was his idea—he was a news film photographer for Channel 11—to put together a thirty-minute documentary on the Southern Crescent for his television station. The train's future is in doubt. Southern Railway wants to orphan it to Amtrak.

Jimmy Harmon went to work with John Pruitt, the new man at Channel 11 who was lured away from Channel 2. They took the long ride up and down the Southern line together.

John Pruitt was telling me Wednesday, "I didn't know anything about trains, but Jimmy did. He was a train freak. He could tell me what kind of diesels were pulling the train. I didn't even know that train Arlo Guthrie sings about, the 'City of New Orleans,' was a real train. Jimmy told me it was, an Illinois Central train."

The documentary will be aired as planned on Channel 11 sometime in September. It will be dedicated to Jimmy Harmon—news photographer, husband, father—who died Wednesday trying to make the product just a little better.

From a number of sources, here is what likely happened to him:

The filming of the documentary was actually completed. But he had been out each morning this week, trying for even more foot-age of the train's arrival in Atlanta.

Wednesday morning, there was fog in Atlanta. Jimmy Harmon may have envisioned a shot of the Southern Crescent rolling out of that fog.

He set up two cameras on a relatively new trestle that crosses North Druid Hills Road near Peachtree Road in DeKalb County.

One camera, a sound camera, was rolling at one side of the tracks where the train would soon pass. A silent camera, small enough to be embedded in the gravel between the tracks, would perhaps pick up a dramatic shot of the train roaring directly over it.

There are two buttons to be pushed to activate the silent cam-era. One button starts the camera. The other locks it into the "on" position.

Jimmy Harmon apparently tried to wait until the last moment before the train's arrival from around a curve to activate his camera.

He moved too slowly. The engineer of the train said he was directly in front of the huge diesel when he was swept underneath the train and dragged 600 feet.

"I've just come to work here," John Pruitt was saying, "and I hadn't really known Jimmy that long. But we worked closely to-gether on the documentary. I feel like I've lost my best friend."

They called Jimmy Harmon a "damn good photographer" at 11. They talked about the grief of his wife, Donna, his son, Cary, twelve, and his daughter, Shana, six. They were working at the station to produce for the evening news broadcasts a sensitive goodby to one of their own.

A little boy never lost his love for trains. Wednesday, in the line of duty, it killed him.

The Smiling Chef

Yeah, I knew Lewis Price. I have eaten his cooking, and I have shaken his hand. And what comes back now is the recollection of the morning I poked my sleepy head into his office—the kitchen of the Southern Crescent passenger train dining car—and inquired as to the state of his general health and well-being.

We were northbound, a few hours out of Washington. He had been up for hours and busy every minute. He made his own bran muffins for breakfast, a South Crescent speciality.

He replied to my inquiry, smiling. "Everything is beautiful, Cap'n. Everything is beautiful." The man used all his face when he smiled.

He went to work as a chef on the Southern in 1941, and for thirty-seven years to come, he would practice his arts midst the grease and smoke and crowded dining-car kitchen facilities.

Company executives, the story goes, often tried to lure him away from the passengers to their private cars. And once he left the rails altogether to become chef at the Alabama governor's mansion. He could cook, understand.

But he was back on the trains shortly. "Too many female bosses" is why Lewis Price said he departed Montgomery.

He died Sunday morning. Lewis Price, sixty-four and a native of Athens and a resident of Atlanta, was one of six people killed when the Southern Crescent left the tracks in Virginia shortly before dawn on its daily Atlanta-to-Washington run.

The smiling chef—wearing his starched white frock—was preparing breakfast when the crash occurred.

The photographs of the wreck were horrible. Twisted cars strewn about the tracks. I make a habit of riding the Southern Crescent. I might have been in the dining car talking to Lewis Price.

He leaves a widow. He leaves five children—the youngest a daughter enrolled at Georgia State—and five grandchildren.

Larry Price is one of his sons. He is twenty-nine and a real estate developer. He was at his father's Burbank Drive home Monday, awaiting news of when his father's body would be returned from Virginia.

"We waited all day Sunday to hear the inevitable," he said. "Finally, at about six o'clock in the evening, we heard the news."

I asked him to talk about his father. He complied without further persuasion.

"He had an eighth-grade education," Larry Price began. "And what he wanted most was for his children to have the education, the independence, the chances he never had.

"When he went to work for the railroad, black people didn't have that many choices. But he liked the railroad, and he worked hard at his job because he wanted to provide for his family.

"And he did provide. We never lived in Sandy Springs or anything like that, but we never wanted for much, either. We were never hungry. We were never cold. And we never went barefooted.

"I never heard him talk about it, but I suppose he thought something like this could happen. There is always that chance.

"All his children were close to him. He taught us to have pride in ourselves. He instilled that in us. And he made us happy."

The Southern Crescent's future is in doubt, of course. Southern Railway wants to discontinue the train because of heavy operating losses.

"That bothered my father," Larry Price said. "He was thinking about retiring early because of it. I think he would have retired next year if the train had been stopped."

I will remember Lewis Price mostly for his smile and his food and the fact he was a vanishing breed. Passenger trains and the people who made them the Grand Conveyance of another time are running thirty years behind schedule and losing ground.

"All my father would want," the son said, "is to be remembered as loyal to the Southern Crescent. It was his life."

Engine Ride

ABOARD THE SOUTHERN CRESCENT — This weirdo little kid I know who loves passenger trains and wouldn't give you a dime for what the Wright Brothers thought was such a big deal got to ride in the head engine of the Southern Crescent twice this week.

North to Greenville, South Carolina, in the evening, and south back to Atlanta early the next morning.

I went along as a sort of chaperon.

It was the kid's last opportunity to experience such an adventure. Wednesday night, Southern Railway got out of the passenger train business, 149 years after it began, when the last Southern Crescent pulled out of Atlanta's Peachtree Station bound for Washington, D. C.

As of Thursday, Amtrak controls Atlanta's only passenger train. It is now called, simply, "The Crescent," and even its future may be limited.

This kid should have his head examined. Once he paid $50 for a conductor's hat. He wears it when he listens to his record of train sounds. He has pictures of trains on his walls, and once he even spent a honeymoon night on a train.

He's a mature kid.

He climbed up the side of the green and gold Southern engine Number 6914 shortly before 7:30 P.M. at Peachtree Station, and he heard the conductor from the back of the train, "Train Number Two, the blue flag is down! Let's leave here!"

He remembered to go to the bathroom before his trip began. That is important for a little kid because riding in the engine of a passenger train is very exciting.

He got to sit next to the engineer and watch him pull back the throttle and turn on the air brakes and blow the whistle of the ancient, snorting diesel when school buses approached crossings.

There are fifty-two crossings between Atlanta and the train's first stop, Gainesville. The whistle must be blown before reaching each one. Two long blows. One short. Another long.

That is 208 pulls on the train whistle the first hour of the trip.

"I love my job," said the engineer, "But people at crossings will drive you crazy. I fear school buses and tank trucks. In that order."

Occasionally, people attempt to beat trains across road crossings. Occasionally, they don't make it and get themselves wiped out.

The enginer's name was M.D. Hester, a man steady-handed,

clear-eyed, and steel-jawed. He wore a green baseball cap and said he has been at his job for thirty-nine years, the last six of which have been spent driving the Southern Crescent between Atlanta and Greenville.

He will continue to drive the train for Amtrak "until I get disgusted." You know how working for the govenment can be.

A passenger train engineer stays busy. He reads signals that tell him which track to take because there is a freight train on the other one. He reads orders to tell him now how fast to run the train.

His maximum speed on curves is sixty miles per hour. His maximum speed on straight track is seventy-nine. In December, the Southern Crescent ran off the track in Virginia because the train was going too fast for a curve. Six people died.

A foreman in the engine explained how that happened. The engineer had sent the fireman, his co-pilot, back into the engine because of a power malfunction.

Alone in the cab, the engineer was busy with controls at his back and did not notice he had reached the curve at a speed of eighty miles an hour. Once he realized his mistake, he attempted to brake the train. When he applied the emergency braking system, the second engine came off the tracks and all hell broke loose.

Human error, they call it.

M.D. Hester was driving the Southern Crescent into Atlanta one morning and hit a local television cameraman filming his train. The cameraman was killed.

It wasn't Mr. Hester's fault, but he doesn't want to talk about it, other than to say he still has trouble sleeping at night.

He did say, however, the person driving the train is often in danger, too.

"We're sitting ducks up here," he explained. "People throw things off overpasses and hang things off overpasses for us to hit. Once I hit a concrete block hanging from a rope off an overpass."

Why aren't people who would do things like that in institutions?

"You never know what you will see," the engineer went on. "One morning I was coming in and a man appeared at the side of the train. He wore a hat he had made out of honeysuckles, a pair of clodhoppers and nothing else.

"He ran along the side of the train, flapping his arms trying to fly." Probably somebody late for work at the state capitol.

We were thirty-four minutes behind schedule leaving Atlanta for Greenville. You cross Piedmont Road, then Interstate 285, on and on out through Duluth and Buford and Flowery Branch.

We whisked past Bill Miner's Crossing, named for the last person to hold up a Southern Railway passenger train. That was 1907. He got $18,000 in gold but was captured a few days later, passed out drunk in a Dahlonega hotel room.

There is a downhill glide into Toccoa, taken at a smooth sixty, and there is a tall trestle to cross over the river into South Carolina.

Clemson is a flagstop. More than the normal number of passengers boarded the train at the old station in Greenville, northbound for such places as Charlotte, Greensboro, Danville, Lynchburg, and finally, Washington, at shortly past eight the next morning.

The sun rises on the southbound Southern Crescent in the still-icy hills of Banks, Habersham and Hall. Greeting morning in the engine of a passenger train, with three other engines behind you making the noise of the devils of 10,000 hells, is something Freud should have experienced and interpreted.

The little kid loved every minute of it. When we had left the engine back at Peachtree Station, I asked him what he thought of Brock Adams, Jimmy Carter's secretary of transportation, who is trying to do away with 10,000 miles of the Amtrak system, including the route of the Crescent.

"Why doesn't he go to lunch with a highway construction lobbyist and leave the rest of us alone?" the little kid asked back.

I didn't have an answer for him.

Besides, his eyes were still wide and his heart was still pounding from what the engineer had allowed him to do as the train had approached the station moments before.

He let the little kid blow the whistle, on the Southern Crescent.

And his life was complete.

Saying Goodby

ABOARD THE SOUTHERN CRESCENT — I don't know exactly where we were. Between Spartanburg and Charlotte perhaps. Midnight approached. Four hours earlier, the Southern Crescent had pulled out of Atlanta's Peachtree Station bound for Washington with three green-and-gold engines, thirteen cars and a pack of riders come to attend the funeral-on-wheels of America's last privately owned overnight luxury passenger train.

"I just wanted to say goodby in person," said a man who had boarded in Gainesville for a half hour ride to Toccoa.

There were three of them. The big one had a full beard, and he wore a cowboy hat. Somebody said his daddy was a big wheel with Southern Railway. You could have fooled me.

From somewhere in the back of the train they had each pulled out a guitar, and the music they were making had hushed what moments before had been a noisy, close-to-rowdy crowd that had gathered in the lounge car to drink its final respects to the Southern Crescent.

A black man and a black woman wearing white starched coats in the South tradition, poured.

Train songs. Naturally we wanted train songs. The guitar trio obliged. The big one with the hat and beard had a voice on him.

They began with "The Glendale Train." Somebody robbed it. They played "City of New Orleans," of course, and everybody sang along.

People took pictures. Channel 5 rolled its film. A girl got drunk and suggested we all greet the waiting passengers in Charlotte with a group "moon." The vote was close against her. A passenger ordered more beer for the singers, and I was in the middle of thanking the Lord for letting me be there when in walked Graham Claytor.

Graham Claytor is secretary of the Navy. Before Jimmy Carter gave him that job, he was president of Southern Railway and a fine friend to people who like to ride in passenger trains.

It was Graham Claytor who had insisted that the Southern Crescent continue running—and continue its excellence of service —when all others around him wanted it stopped. He was a paying passenger this night, however. He had his own goodbys to say.

The big one cut down on "Wreck of Old '97," a damn fine train song, and Mr. Secretary of the Navy Claytor soloed to the top of his voice.

It was a poignant moment in the storied history of railroading.

He lingered with the passengers after his song. He even signed autographs, and he assured those who asked that Amtrak, which assumed control of the Southern Crescent Thursday, would continue the train's branch of service.

"This isn't the end of anything," Graham Claytor said.

But the Department of Transportation Secretary Brock Adams has proposed doing away with even the Amtrak version of the train.

"I don't think that will happen," said Claytor. "The political reality is this train will continue."

Another round for the singers, please.

Southern's plush office car number 11, fit for the company brass it carried, brought up the rear of the train Wednesday night. Atlantan Jack Martin, a power in the National Association of Railroad Passengers—the group that would like to hang Brock Adams —was on board. And somebody said they spotted Marvin Hamlisch. Marvin Hamlisch, among other things, wrote the music for *A Chorus Line.*

There were reporters and photographers and television people. And a group from Atlanta that would ride northbound to Salisbury, North Carolinia, and then return on the final southbound Southern Crescent at 2:30 in the morning.

One Atlanta man had ridden the train from Atlanta to New Orleans Tuesday then boarded again Wednesday morning for the full trip back to Washington.

"It's my birthday present to myself," he said.

Southern also had extra security on the train. That was to keep souvenir-seeking passengers from stripping it. Extra security didn't help that much. Menus disappeared by the dozens from tables in the dining car.

So did napkins and coasters, and a sleeping-car porter was missing his platform stool.

"My God," said a conductor, "I'm glad the toilets are bolted down."

There was one ugly incident. A young woman who had driven from Jacksonville to Atlanta to ride the train had her purse stolen. Security men finally located the culprit in a dark coach. They retrieved the purse and put the thief off the train in the cold and dark of Greensboro, North Carolina, at 3 in the morning, which is exactly what he deserved.

The Southern Crescent had been ten minutes late in arriving in Atlanta from New Orleans. With maybe a couple of hundred standing in the cold night to watch. The train finally poked its nose around the corner, gave a blast of its horn, and there was scattered applause.

"It's a sad day," said a man taking pictures.

Over the Peachtree Station loudspeaker came the Southern Crescent's final call. The caller sang it out: "Here comes the Southern Crescent, all the way from New Orleeeens!"

He added, "Thank you for riding Southern all these years." A touch of class.

All these years were 149 of them. Southern Railway opened regularly scheduled passenger service in the United States in 1830. The Southern Crescent was born the Washington and Southwestern Vestibuled Limited in January of 1893. Timetables advertised trips to Atlanta, the "Queen City of the New South."

Gainesville was the first stop Wednesday night. Then Toccoa, Clemson, Greenville, Spartanburg, Gastonia, Charlotte, Salisbury, High Point, Greensboro, Danville, Lynchburg, Charlottesville, Culpeper, Alexandria and finally across the Potomac River into cold and windy Washington and Union Station. Twenty minutes later than the advertised 8:50 A.M.

There were no bands, no speeches. The train pulled in. The train stopped. The people got out. An era passed.

I own a book called *A Portrait of the Rails.* A man named David Morgan wrote the introduction. As I left the Southern Crescent for the last time Thursday morning, I thought about a line from that introduction.

The unmatched adventure of rail and steel is nearly over. I admit that. So does David Morgan. But at least he sounded hopeful when he wrote, "Oh, Lord, but it will take some doing for America to get that adventure out of her soul."

AIN'T LOVE GRAND?

Somewhere in this chapter is a column that expresses my feelings about homemade biscuits and their relationship to love and marriage. You would think a column like that would not make anybody mad.

You would think wrong. They came at me with hatpins. One militant women's rights group wanted to chase me down Peachtree Street with large sticks.

I have always considered myself an expert on women's liberation. In the last fifteen years, I have given two their freedom myself.

Valentine's Day Massacre

This may be an inappropriate time to break such news. Then, again, today is Valentine's, and this is a love story, or what's left of it.

It began when I was in the third grade. So was my boyhood friend and idol, Weyman C. Wannamaker Jr., a great American.

The summer break had passed, and it was the first day of the new school year. We were standing, Weyman and I, by the playground swing set where Weyman ran a thriving porno business.

Weyman's older brother was in the Navy. He came home on leave and brought Weyman a deck of playing cards with pictures you didn't see that often in those timid times.

For a dime, you got a blind draw out of Weyman's deck, and you didn't have to give the card back until lunch period. Weyman sold out almost every morning, and by the time the cards and pictures were too worn for further rentals, he had a downpayment on a movie projector, which is another story.

"There's a new girl in our class," Arnold Bates walked up and told us. Arnold, who was one of Weyman's best customers, got all the inside information at school because his mother taught sixth grade.

Arnold also wore thick glasses and got extra dessert in the lunchroom. "Arnold ain't worth killing" is what Weyman thought of him.

This time, however, Weyman was keenly interested in what Arnold had to say. I knew that because when Arnold wouldn't tell him the new girl's name unless Weyman rented him his favorite card for free, Weyman belted him one.

"Kathy Sue Loudermilk," said Arnold, picking himself up off the playground dirt. You didn't make deals with the third grade godfather.

It was love at first sight. Weyman already had a stable of grade-school lovelies that even included a fifth-grader, Margie Round-tree, who wore lipstick and was talked about in faculty meetings.

"She's headed for nothing but trouble," is what Arnold Bates said his mother heard the principal say about her. Weyman simply wanted to be there when she arrived.

But there was something special about Kathy Sue Loudermilk. Even at eight, she made a tight sweater seem much more than a woolen garment.

I had never seen Weyman act as he did over the new girl in class. He brought her candy. He walked her home from school every day. He tried to break Arnold Bates' arm for talking to her during morning recess. He even offered her one of his playing cards for half price. Weyman was *delirious* with love.

As the years passed, nothing changed. When Weyman was sixteen, he bought his first car, a 1953 Ford. He covered the backseat with a chenille bedspread, put shag carpets on the floorboard, and hung a pair of foam rubber dice from the rearview mirror.

It was in this romantic setting that they spent evening after evening parked in the pecan grove behind the Line Creek Fundamental Back-to-the-Bible Church.

One night the preacher dropped by the church to prepare his Sunday sermon. He caught Weyman and Kathy Sue as they were about to drive away. The lint on her skirt was a dead giveaway.

"My children," asked the preacher, "have you sinned?"

"I don't know about her," said Weyman, "but I did all I could."

Nobody knows the real reason they never married. Weyman

bought a truck and went into the produce business. Kathy Sue had already filled out her ambitions by the time she was out of high school. They retired her sweater when she graduated.

Weyman called the other day. I could tell something was wrong.

"Hear about Kathy Sue?" he asked.

I hadn't.

"Ran off and got married," Weyman said.

"I'm sorry," is all I could think to say. "Anybody I know?"

"Arnold Bates," Weyman answered, choking back the tears. He was sacking a load of onions at the time.

He will eventually get over the hurt, of course. Not Weyman. Arnold. Weyman went on to mention he had given the happy groom a wedding present. They'll take the cast off in six weeks.

Charlie and Julia

I called the Atlanta federal pen to inquire about Charlie Hines, Number 31579-120. Charlie, who is sixty-four, robbed a bank down in Florida a couple of years ago. After his conviction, he was shipped off to the "Big A."

"Yep," said a most unpleasant voice on the other end of the phone, "we still got 'im."

And probably will have for some time to come.

Charlie sent me something in the mail once. It was a copy of an article by a *Florida Times-Union* reporter named Ken Cruickshank. The article explained how Charlie became a bank robber.

I'll take the story from Cruickshank's article. He said he didn't mind.

Charlie got married in 1968 to a lady named Julia. Cruickshank told me, "They were a very devoted couple."

But hard times soon followed the marriage. Charlie had trouble with his feet. He was a diabetic. He had managed an amusement park in Tampa, but his health forced him to quit.

He bought some property in Tampa and opened a tavern and restaurant.

But Charlie Hines was in and out of the hospital and was eventually declared disabled by the Social Security Administration. He and his wife were trying to live on $156 a month.

In 1973 their problems worsened. Julia had to have an operation for cancer.

Charlie tried to go back to work to pay for her medicine. He tried a paper route of 125 miles for eleven months. Because of his health, he lost money on the route and was forced to quit again.

The bank took the tavern and restaurant away. Charlie turned sixty-two. His disability payments stopped. Social Security payments started. Now, Charlie and Julia Hines were trying to live on $137.10 a month.

Julia was in terrible pain, the story continues. Her medicine was expensive. Liquor was cheap. She began drinking heavily.

"I would mix her a drink to ease her," Charlie told Ken Cruickshank. "That's how it started."

Charlie's condition hadn't improved, either. He was having dizzy spells and periodic blackouts. A doctor ordered a brain scan.

"I couldn't do it, though," Charlie explained. "I didn't have that kind of money."

It was May 1977 and Charlie Hines was desperate. He borrowed a .22 pistol and took five times his normal amount of pain-killers—"so I could walk"—and went out to look for a bank to rob.

He found one in Inverness, Florida. Charlie doesn't know exactly how much money he took. He never got a chance to count it. He was captured an hour later, fifteen miles away. He tried to plead insanity, but the jury wouldn't listen.

"I thought I was dying anyway," he said. "We had no food, no money and no prospect of getting any. So I went in and robbed that bank."

Last I heard, Charlie hadn't seen his wife since his interview with Ken Cruickshank. She can't come for visits.

Julia Hines, who accompanied her husband everywhere, was outside in the car that day while Charlie was inside robbing the bank.

Her number, incidentally, is 01129-179, Women's Unit, Lexington, Kentucky. She got fifteen months.

What made me think of Charlie and Julia was the exciting news that heiress Patty Hearst, who was also convicted of robbing a bank, had been freed from prison in time for her upcoming wedding to her former bodyguard.

It may be "the biggest wedding California has ever seen," said one news story, or just a "simple, private ceremony."

Whatever, they can afford it.

Let's all wish the happy couple well.

Lovin' in the Oven

Jerry Clower, the funniest man alive, does a routine on one of his records about biscuits. Jerry says the absence of homemade biscuits at the American breakfast table is one reason the divorce rate is going up.

"Saddest sound in this world," Jerry once told me, "is the sound of them little canned biscuits being popped open early evah mawnin' in evah house in the neighborhood."

Jerry goes, "Whop! Whop! Whop!" as an illustration. It's enough to make a grown man cry.

I agree with Jerry Clower. Give a man homemade biscuits in the morning, and he'll come home to you at night. The Pillsbury Doughboy, with his dratted canned biscuits, is a lousy home-wrecker.

There was a time, especially in the South, when the woman arose early enough in the morning to prepare homemade biscuits for her husband and family. It was a simpler time. Before mixed doubles replaced sex.

Women in those days served plates of piping hot biscuits. Big, fluffy biscuits. Cut one open. Slap a portion of butter between the halves and then cover that with your choice of jam or jelly.

"A breakfast without biscuits," went a famous saying, "is like a day without sunshine."

But what, if anything, endures? The last homemade biscuit I saw was in a museum behind a glass case.

It is time, women of America, to come to your senses. Halt the alarming increase in the divorce rate! Bring the homemade biscuit back to your breakfast table! We can all work together! You make 'em, we'll eat 'em. What could be more fair?

I must insist on taking a hard line on this matter. Any woman within the range of this column who subsequently serves her family canned biscuits for breakfast in anything but an extreme emergency is a brazen hussy who smokes filterless cigarettes, drinks beer from a can and doesn't shave her legs.

I called the editor of a famous cookbook, *A Taste of Georgia,* for help. She lives in Newnan and later this month, she is taking her book to the White House to present a copy to Rosalynn Carter.

A Taste of Georgia is in homes all over the country, including Alaska, where the Eskimos are now eating grits with their whale blubber. The book contains thousands of Deep South recipes, including some for biscuits.

The editor of *A Taste of Georgia* is Mrs. White. Mrs. John N. White. *Martha* White. I swear.

"It's not that hard to make biscuits in the morning," said Martha White. "It's just that it takes a lot of time. Most women these days simply don't want to spend that much time in the kitchen in the morning when there are so many other options open to them."

Like watching "Donahue"? Like playing in the Wednesday Morning Serve and Chat Doubles? Like running for political office? Like marching on a nuclear plant?

I accept no excuses, and there is nothing uglier than a hairy-legged girl. I asked Martha White if she cooked biscuits in the mornings for her family.

"Not on weekdays," she said. "Besides, my husband doesn't like a big breakfast."

Mr. White could not be reached for comment.

I looked in *A Taste of Georgia* for a biscuit recipe. One is for "Angel Biscuits."

You need flour, baking soda, salt, baking powder, sugar, shortening, yeast and buttermilk. Cook for twelve minutes. Sounds divine.

And one more thing, an ingredient most important. The last woman to cook biscuits for me in the mornings was a lady I lived with for seventeen years. I can remember asking her, "What makes these biscuits so good?"

"Love, son," she would say. "I put in lots of love."

Homemade biscuits for breakfast, ladies? At least once? And soon?

He'll taste the love. I promise.

Making Up

I remain convinced love conquers all, even in this day and time of rampant divorces and the breakdown of the family.

Take the recent example of the lovely Oregon couple, John and Greta Rideout. Greta called the cops on her husband one day and claimed he had raped her.

John said everybody knows you can't rape your own wife. That would be like stealing your own car.

A messy and much-publicized trial resulted. Besides raping her, Greta said, another thing she didn't like about her husband was he didn't keep his fingernails trimmed and clean. John countered and said Greta had these weirdo sexual fantasies that didn't include him.

Luckily for husbands everywhere, the jury said, "Not guilty."

But that was not the end of the story. Almost before the jury could get out of its box, Greta and John announced they had resolved their differences and were returning home to live as husband and wife.

If John and Greta Rideout can patch things up again, anybody can. Including the Marietta couple that was divorced last week.

I couldn't believe my eyes as I read news reports of what finally put their marriage asunder. It happened last October. On Halloween night.

There stood the wife, who was separted from her husband at the time, minding her own business in her kitchen. Into the room walked the muscular figure of the man she married.

He's an avid weightlifter, so the story goes. Apparently, that's not all of his problem.

He was dressed in the costume of the televison character, the "Incredible Hulk," all green and scary looking. On television, the "Incredible Hulk" is a quiet, unassuming, puny physicist who has this chemical imbalance in his body.

When riled, the physicist swells to several times his normal size, and his face changes into something that would scare a dog off a meat wagon.

Frightening his wife right out of her apron wasn't enough for the Cobb Clonker, by day a pharmacist.

According to the news story, he also pounded his wife one to the head, rendering her unconscious as they say at police head-quarters.

He denied belting her and said he had simply dropped by her kitchen on his way to a Halloween party where he later won "best costume" after eating the glass punch bowl.

The divorce was granted last week. I called authorities in Cobb County for further details. I was told the man is presently free on a $3,000 peace bond following another assault on his wife.

I also found out policemen hate dealing with this sort of situation because it can be extremely dangerous duty.

"What drives us crazy," a Cobb officer said, "is when you go into one of these things where the man has beaten up his old lady and she wants him thrown in jail, sometimes she'll turn on you if you have to take him out by force.

"These officers went into a house one night. The woman was all bloody and bruised. Two or three young'uns were crying, and the man was drunk. They tried to take him to jail, and he put up a fight.

"Before you knew it, the woman and the young'uns were breaking things over the officer's heads. They knocked the brim clean off one officer's Stetson."

That's what I was saying. When the going gets tough, love can still overcome the greatest obstacles. I think there is definite hope for the ex-couple from Marietta.

He wants to be the "Incredible Hulk." Fine. She could dress up like "Wonder Woman." Give and take. That's the answer.

Just like the Rideouts. John is going to get a manicure, and Greta, sweet thing, has promised to try to work him into at least two fantasies a week.

My Little Cupcake

Dear "Sweetie-Poo,"

Bet you thought you'd never hear me call you that again. Cupcake, we may be living apart now, but there are some things I will never forget about the six weeks we had together.

Just the other day, I was remembering how I started calling you that name, "Sweetie Poo." Do you remember, Dovey? I used to leave little notes on my pillow before I left for work so you would find them when you awakened later.

I would write, "Roses are red, violets are blue, and I love my Sweetie-Poo." I know you enjoyed them because you would always call me the minute you turned over and found them.

I'm sorry I was hardly ever in the office when you called, but the boss insisted we knock off for lunch at one o'clock on the dot.

Darling, I've been doing a lot of thinking about what happened to our Little Blue Heaven. I have never had a shock like the one you gave me when you said you believed we should separate and I should move out because marriage was stifling your career.

Honey, I still believe you could be married and teach bridge at the club, too, but I suppose it's too late to turn back now. I guess you know your lawyer has talked to mine and we'll be going to court soon to get the divorce.

Maybe you didn't know. I ran into your best friend Gladys, and she said you've been traveling a lot. Aspen, huh? I'll bet you turned a few heads on the slopes with those new ski outfits you bought for the trip.

Didn't think I knew about that, did you, Pumpkin? The bill you had the department store send me came this morning. We've worked something out so I can pay a little at the time. It probably helped that your old man owns the joint.

Incidentally, if Gladys mentions anything about my saying I hoped you broke you leg in five places, I was only kidding, *ma chérie*.

Drove by the house the other night to pick up the broom and dustpan set you gave me as a wedding present, but I was afraid to come in. It looked like you might be having a party.

The band sounded tremendous. I know you are going to think I'm crazy, but for a moment, I thought I could see you and your lawyer dancing without any clothes on by the pool. Silly me. Just my imagination, I'm sure, or the lighting from the Japanese lanterns.

By the way, was that a new car I saw parked in the driveway? Gladys also said something about your Dad giving you a new Jag to help you get over the grief of our sudden breakup.

Love that color! You always did look good in red. Besides, the burnt orange Porsche he gave you for your birthday last month simply wasn't you, Cutes.

Sorry I got so upset last month when you said you had run out of money again and I'd have to make the house payment. I had some fool notion you could put what I send you together with the allowance from your old man and have plenty for the mortgage and some left over.

But you're right. I had no idea the price of tennis outfits had gone up so much, and I didn't know your father had cut you to a grand a week because of the way his stocks have fallen off.

I managed to scrape by. The watch my grandfather gave me on his deathbed was worth a pretty penny at the pawn shop, and I sold a few pints of blood to get the rest.

I'm doing just fine in my new place, Gumdrop. The landlord said he couldn't do anything about the rats for a while, but I'm getting used to them. It's nice to have some pleasant company for a change. (Ha! Ha! Still kidding, my little Sweet Potato.)

Better close for now, Puddin.' Know you're busy. Me, too. Working two jobs can sure keep a fellow hopping. One more thing, I really laughed when Gladys made that crack about you and your lawyer planning to "take me to the cleaners" in divorce court. You're a regular riot, Loveykins.

All for now. Write soon.

Always,

Your "Precious Lamb"

P.S.: My lawyer just called and told me the Supreme Court has ruled that women with a lot money may now have to pay alimony to their husbands.

P.P.S. See you in court, Snorkel-Face.

Hope

ELLIJAY — The day has grown old gracefully in Ellijay, where the mountains are about to begin, and as is the custom in such settings, men with nothing better to do have gathered around the courthouse. In this case, it is the Gilmer County courthouse. There is a tree in front. And benches.

I still love a courthouse because it was on the steps of one I learned to play checkers and dominoes, and I learned about the Book of Revelation, which is what the old men would talk about after they tired of checkers and dominoes.

"Gon' be an awful day That Day," one old man would say at the courthouse.

"Gon' be a lot of folks caught short That Day," another would reply.

I even tried to read Revelation once. I stopped. It spooked me.

Standing with the men under the tree in front of the Gilmer County courthouse, I noticed the heat again—it remained stifling despite the approaching dusk—and perhaps that is what brought back Revelation's fiery warnings so vividly.

I am in Ellijay to watch the campaign tactics of Mary Beth Busbee, wife of the governor who is the first man in our state's modern history to seek a second consecutive term to that post.

I watch her closely and decide she loves her husband deeply or she wouldn't be working with such fervor. That feels good to me. He is campaigning south. She is campaigning north. Mary Beth Busbee says to people, "I'm Mary Beth Busbee, and I hope you will vote for my husband."

As I watch her, I think about marriage and how it has failed me —or how I have failed it—and I wonder if there is hope for those of us who have seen only marriage's bad side.

Earlier, Mary Beth Busbee had walked into a book and magazine store on the Ellijay courthouse square. "I'm Mary Beth Busbee," she said to the woman working there, "and I hope you will vote for my husband."

The woman spoke up quickly, "I lost my husband, you know. A year ago. He had a massive heart attack."

Mrs. Busbee listened. The woman's voice cracked with emotion. A year later, her voice still cracked with emotion.

The governor's wife introduced herself to the group standing at the courthouse.

A man in a T-shirt said, "If I was runnin' for office, the last person I'd want out tryin' to get me votes is my wife."

Mrs. Busbee wanted to know why.

" 'Cause," the man went on, "She ain't never said nothin' good about me at home, and I know she ain't gonna say nothin' good about me out in public."

That brought a laugh all around. A good marriage needs a little levity, I was thinking.

Grady was there, and he met Mrs. Busbee, too. Grady is wearing overalls. His hat is twice my age. Remnants of the day's snuff encircle his mouth. For every courthouse, there is a Grady.

"Grady's ninety-three," somebody said.

"He still gets up and preaches over at the Holiness Church," somebody else said.

"That's my wife over there," Grady said to me. I looked and

saw a little lady in a print dress, sitting on one of the benches alone. She drank water from a tall soft-drink bottle. There was evidence she dips now and then, too.

"How long you been married?" I asked Grady.

"Twelve years," he answered. "She's a good woman."

As I drove from Ellijay, I looked back once at the courthouse. Grady and his bride were walking away. It may have been my imagination, but I think I saw him take her hand.

Only one thing spooks me more than Revelation. Marriage. But Mary Beth loves George, a woman in a store grieves a year later, a husband makes a loving joke, and a ninety-three-year-old newly-wed still feels the spark.

There is hope. There *is* hope.

• 10 •

A STINKING PLACE TO DIE

A good father. A good son. A good cop. A good friend. And a porno hustler who saw the light. Death and near-death from Guyana to Lawrenceville, Georgia.

Don Harris

Ray Tapley is a man I have known for a long time. He has a good job with an insurance company in Atlanta, but he continues to insist upon working for the newspaper on Saturday nights.

Ray Tapley writes headlines and edits stories that appear in the Sunday sports section.

Saturday night, he said he only glanced at the front page when the final Sunday edition came up to the newsroom for a final read-down.

"I saw the headlines about Congressman Ryan possibly being killed in Guyana," Ray said, "but I didn't look at the story any closer. Only after I got home and read the entire report did I know about Don Harris.

"And it took me a minute to recall 'Don Harris' was Darwin Humphrey's television name."

Don Harris—or Darwin Humphrey—was the NBC reporter from Los Angeles who was murdered along with Rep. Leo J. Ryan, two other newsmen and a member of the suicidal People's Temple settlement in the Saturday ambush at Port Kaituma, Guyana.

I am still not certain where Guyana is, or even *what* it is, but I do know it is a million miles from Vidalia, Georgia, and one stinking place to die.

Darwin Humphrey was from Vidalia, down Route 297 off Inter-

state 16, in the heart of tobacco country. Vidalia is 11–12,000
people. Ray Tapley says it is the largest town between Dublin and
Savannah. He also says it is the largest town in Georgia—outside a
metro area—that is not a county seat. Lyons keeps the courthouse
in Toombs County.

Ray is also from Vidalia. He and Darwin Humphrey used to ride
the school bus together thirty years ago.

"Both our families lived in the country," Ray Tapley was saying
Tuesday. He would be leaving his office soon to return home to
Vidalia for Thanksgiving. And for Darwin Humphrey's funeral
Wednesday morning.

"His mother always came out on the front porch to see Darwin
when he got on the bus in the morning and when he got off in the
afternoon."

Later, Ray Tapley's family and Darwin Humphrey's family—
there were two younger brothers—both moved into Vidalia, country folks come to town. They settled around the corner from each
other. "I saw Darwin grow up," Ray said. "He was only fifteen
when he started announcing for our radio station. They were a
middle-class family, good people. His father worked behind the
vegetable counter at the supermarket."

Darwin Humphrey left Vidalia for Statesboro and Georgia
Southern. He had a radio job while in school. Then, it was
Charleston and a stop here and a stop there and a name change to a
more flattering-for-television "Don Harris," and on to Los Angeles
and NBC.

And finally to that airstrip in Guyana where a shotgun blast
ended his life. He was forty-two, the father of three.

There is more about Darwin Humphrey. His speech teacher at
the high school in Vidalia says that in twenty-five years, he was her
most gifted student. Another is a New York actress.

Both his younger brothers followed him into radio careers. A
daughter—Claire, sixteen—has lived in Los Angeles for five years.
She says, "Vidalia is my home."

I talked to Claire Humphrey Tuesday afternoon at her grandmother's house in Vidalia. She says she is proud of her daddy.

"He was always leaving, we were used to that," she explained. Her voice was strong. "We knew what he was going to do was dangerous, but he did other dangerous things. We expected him back in a week.

"He was a very brave man. We are proud of him."

I don't know if Darwin Humphrey was aware of it before he died, but his daughter told me something Tuesday that would have made him proud.

"My brother is seventeen," she said. Her brother's name is Jeff. And he has already decided upon his future.

"He wants to be a television reporter," said Claire. "Like his father was."

Jesse Frank Frosch

Jesse Frank Frosch of Speedway, Indiana, was twenty-seven when he died. We had both struggled together on a struggling daily newspaper in Athens, and I looked up to him because he was a genius.

Frank Frosch was a brilliant writer. Once he wrote a story about what it's like in his hometown the night before the Indianapolis 500 automobile race.

That story remains the best sports story I have ever read.

Besides teaching English at the University of Georgia, Frank also led the band at a rural high school near Athens. He was well qualified to do that because he played something like thirty musical instruments.

Frank raised dogs, too. Basset hounds. When they sent Frank off to Vietnam in 1968, he asked me to keep one of his dogs while he was away. The dog's name was "Plato" and his pedigree reached for miles. Frank had paid $500 for the dog.

When he came back from Vietnam, the dog and I had become very close. I was prepared to pay Frank any amount of money to keep "Plato."

That wasn't necessary. Frank gave me to the dog. That's a friend.

Frank Frosch was an Army intelligence officer in Vietnam. He knew all about what had happened at My Lai, and after leaving the Army, he detailed his knowledge in a masterful piece in *Playboy*.

He later went to work for United Press International in the Atlanta bureau. That job bored him. He wanted to go back to Southeast Asia, this time as a reporter.

He got his chance. They would eventually make young Frank Frosch the UPI bureau manager in Phnom Penh, Cambodia. Like I said, he was a genius.

I took "Plato" over to Frank's house in Atlanta a couple of days before he left on his new mission. We sat on his front porch and took turns patting the dog, and I recall asking Frank if it ever occurred to him he could get killed.

"If I do," he laughed, "at least it won't be because a beer truck ran over me on my way to cover a stupid county commission meeting."

There were all sorts of stories about what actually happened to Frank Frosch. There were even rumors maybe Frank knew too much about My Lai and political motives were at the dark bottom of his death.

Nine years later, the details are still sketchy.

Frank was working in his office in Phnom Penh. A report came in of fighting on the outskirts of the city.

Frank grabbed a photographer. They jumped into a Volkswagen and drove out in search of the reported action.

When they didn't return for several hours, other reporters went searching for them.

They found both Frank Frosch and the photographer dead in an open field near their car. They had been shot several times by automatic rifle fire.

There was blood in the car. They had apparently been ambushed.

UPI now gives an annual Frank Frosch award for meritorious service to journalism. And his dog lived a long, full life. One hot day when he was fourteen, "Plato" curled up in a cool creek and died in his sleep.

Why I'm discussing Frank Frosch should be obvious. Another American newsman trying to get a story in a foreign country was murdered Wednesday.

The television film of the cold-blooded execution of ABC's Bill Stewart in Managua was sickening. He was unarmed. He was helpless. And some animal kicked him and then blew his head off at point-blank range.

The list of American correspondents killed in stinking places like Cambodia, Guyana and Nicaragua grows while the rest of us in this business wrap up our days with tax relief, gasoline shortages and a four-column headline on the Astros' winning streak.

Frank Frosch of UPI. Ron Harris of NBC. Bill Stewart of ABC. And all the others, rest their brave souls.

At least they didn't die because a beer truck ran over them on the way to cover a stupid county commission meeting.

Mournful Silence for Steve Vann

On a cloudy day, spring's first rain approaching, they came by the hundreds to mourn the death of Steve Vann. One of the preachers got up and said, "This is the Christian act of mourning. That is why we are here."

The chapel was packed with people who had known him, who had loved him. Who still did. Perhaps now more than ever. The hallways outside the chapel were also crowded. Those who couldn't find standing room inside waited in silence outside. Grief is rarely loud.

He was seventeen. He was a senior at Lakeside High School in DeKalb County. He was a quarterback on the football team. He lived in an upper middle-class neighborhood. He had a lot of friends. He had parents who gave him their time and their attention and, of course, their love.

Saturday morning, somebody found him dead in a creek.

"There were all sorts of rumors going around," said a classmate at the funeral. "Somebody at first said he had been stabbed. I knew that wasn't true. If Steve had an enemy, I never heard about it."

The county coroner was on television trying to explain it. Steve Vann died of exposure to cold. He was found in creek water that had been below freezing the night before. The temperatures the night before were also below freezing.

Evidence of drugs were found in Steve Vann's body. There was no overdose, but there were drugs.

I talked to more classmates at the funeral.

"I don't guess anybody will really ever know what happened," said one. "He went to a party Friday night, but Steve just wasn't the type to take anything. He might have smoked some grass, most everybody else does; but I can't see him drinking and taking pills."

"Somebody could have slipped him something," added another. "I knew him as well as anybody in school, and he knew better."

The death has been ruled an accident. The most popular conjecture is Steve Vann, because of the drugs, became disoriented, wandered into the creek and remained there—unconscious—until the cold killed him.

Something like this shouldn't happen here, I was telling myself at the funeral. Look around you, I said. This isn't the ghetto. This is suburbia, good life America.

Steve Vann was no mindless punk.

He was an athlete. He was the second-string quarterback, but Lakeside is a state power with a huge student body from which to draw its talent.

"He had the best arm on the team," somebody said. "It hurt him that he wasn't a starter, but he threw a touchdown pass in one of the last games. He must have thrown the ball sixty yards."

But it happened. Steve Vann's death was drug-related. There is no way to hide it.

A young man standing outside the chapel said, between puffs on a cigarette, "If this don't make you think, nothing will."

I could make this a sermon. Parents tell your children. Teachers shout it. Drugs kill. What I had rather do is take you back to the funeral. There can be no more drastic lesson.

There were flowers, always there are flowers, and their scent inside a funeral home is a sickening sweet.

The casket was a metallic blue. There were flowers on top of it. The mother cried hard. The father appeared stunned. Old people hung their heads. Young people stared in disbelief.

An organ played softly. A man sang, "Will the Circle Be Unbroken?" and "I Come to the Garden Alone" and "The Lord's Prayer."

One preacher said, "We are all in shock."

Another said, "This is a great tragedy."

A third said, "He esteemed his elders, he respected his leaders, he was growing into a man of worth."

And at the end, the father walked to the podium and spoke from his breaking heart.

"If any of you are ever in trouble," he told his son's friends, "if any of you need any help, or need to talk, then come to me. This," he went on, looking at the casket before him, "is enough."

God bless him for saying that.

One Year Later: A Father's Pain

The longer I sat and talked with Ed Vann last week, the more I realized what had happened to him since the last time I saw him.

That was at a DeKalb County funeral chapel. He was standing behind a flower-draped casket telling the young people who had gathered there not to take drugs.

Inside the casket was the body of his seventeen-year-old son who had been found dead in a shallow creek one year ago today.

Steve Vann's death shocked the community in which he had lived. He had been an athlete, quarterback at Lakeside High, an upper middle-class suburban school that is an annual football power.

He had scores of friends. The teary young eyes at the funeral home said that. And he was certainly no foggy-brained junkie. He had no prior record of ever having taken drugs.

But evidence of drugs was found in his body. What on earth could have happened?

Conjecture at the time—still undisputed—was Steve Vann had possibly taken some pills at a party he attended the night before his body was found.

Later, because of the effect of the pills, he had become disoriented and had wandered into the tiny creek. Unconscious, he died there from exposure to the wet and cold of the March night.

Ed Vann still isn't satisfied with the investigation of his son's death by police. "Somebody gave my son bad pills," he said last week.

And he will never be satisfied with his performance as a father.

"Maybe Steve needed something to pick him up, maybe he was tired and was being pushed too hard to excel," Ed Vann said. "I did a lot of talking to him, but that was the problem. What I didn't do was listen. Everybody wants to talk to kids. But nobody ever listens to them."

What has happened to Ed Vann is he is haunted by guilt. Unnecessarily so, probably, but the agony that has lingered this long runs deep within him. "Living hell" is what they call this.

He and Steve's mother are no longer living together. He said she has had her own problems coping with their son's death.

Ed Vann has taken a small apartment, one he had already leased to give to his son after his high school graduation.

He writes poems about his son. He carries them with him at all times.

He grasps at every straw. He asked a family friend along when we met last week. The friend claimed to have seen a vision at Steve's funeral.

"I was standing in the back of the chapel," the man said, "and suddenly everything in the chapel disappeared and in its place came another picture.

"I saw a spring day and a green hill. I saw Steve walking up the hill with Christ. When they reached the top of the hill, Steve turned and waved goodbye. Then, they both disappeared over the hill."

Others have seen similar visions, Ed Vann told me. Another friend, he said, claims to have seen his son twice in the past year.

He even attaches significance to the fact his hair, solid gray a year ago, is now getting darker.

"Who ever heard of that?" he asked. "I don't know what is happening here, but all these experiences must mean something."

Ed Vann's emotional plea to his son's friends at the funeral received a great deal of publicity. That bothers him, too. "Ed Vann Joins Fight Against Drugs" is one of the headlines he can recall.

"I don't want that," he said. "My son was a wonderful human being. You wouldn't believe the things his friends have told me he did for them. I'm not the one who should be praised for anything. The good one, my son, is gone."

I didn't have any answers for Ed Vann last week. I don't know what it is to lose a son. But I do know if a person doesn't eventually accept death, no matter how difficult that might be, he will eventually go straight up a wall.

All I can offer is a couple of suggestions. First, let go, Ed. Forget the visions. Forget your guilt and bitterness. They will destroy you.

And what you might do to help purge those feelings is whenever you see a man with his children still by his side, simply remind him to enjoy and cherish every minute of it.

You would probably be surprised how many fathers need that reminder.

Frank Schlatt: Don't Forget

The story didn't make the front page the other day, and I doubt the television stations even bothered with it. It was filled with a lot of legal-beagle mumbo-jumbo, and it didn't have anything to do with the price of oil, cracks in big airliners, or who's running—or not running—for the U.S. Senate.

"Slaton Appeals Ruling," whispered the uninspired headline.

So what? So this:

The story told about Fulton County District Attorney Lewis Slaton's efforts to convince the Georgia Supreme Court to reconsider a ruling it made May 31.

On May 31, the Georgia Supreme Court cited a technicality and overturned the murder conviction and life sentence of somebody named David Burney, Jr.

The court said that when David Burney, Jr. was tried, the trial judge had erroneously disallowed his request to act as his own co-counsel.

The legalese in the story was taxing, but from what I could gather, the trial judge had decided that since David Burney, Jr. already had two defense lawyers, granting him the right to act as his own co-counsel would have led to "undue disruption" of the trial.

District Attorney Slaton said a trial judge has the inherent authority to make decisions like that.

I don't know one end of a gavel from the other, and I would certainly hate to see David Burney, Jr.'s right to a fair trial violated, so I'm not about to take a stand for or against the Georgia Supreme Court's ruling.

After reading the story, however, I did want to bring up three other persons who have a fair stake in all this. They are the ones usually lost in the shuffle in such high-level maneuverings by men carrying law books. They come under the heading of "victims."

They shouldn't be forgotten.

There was Frank R. Schlatt, who was thirty-one. He was an Atlanta policeman. One day he answered a robbery call in a local furniture store.

David Burney, Jr. and three other goons were at the store. One of them blew off Officer Schlatt's head.

I went to his funeral. It was a pretty day and lots of people came. The chapel was packed. Fellow officers wearing white gloves stood at each side of Officer Schlatt's casket.

Somebody blew "Taps." Lester Maddox sat down front. High commissioners and police department czars arrived in limousines.

The preacher talked about what a good life Officer Schlatt had lived. I remember him trying to explain, then, how the Lord could allow such a good man to die. I forget his explanation.

At the graveside later, a policeman said to me, "We'll find the animals who did this, no matter how long it takes."

Then there was Officer Schlatt's widow. She was young and pretty. For a time, she held together well, but then the reality of the moment hit her again, and she cried hard and long.

God, there is nothing that tears at the heart like the sight of a young widow crying.

By her side under the funeral tent that day was Officer Schlatt's little girl.

What a brave little girl, everybody said. She was nine, I think. She fought off her own grief and tried to console her sobbing mother.

There was an American flag on Officer Schlatt's casket. Atop the flag lay a single flower. The little girl had placed it there for her daddy.

For as long as I live, I will never forget the moment an honor guard solemnly folded the flower into the flag and handed it to the grieving widow and daughter.

I don't really have an ending for this. I just wanted to make sure Officer Frank Schlatt and his family were at least mentioned while our judicial system contemplates how it can best serve David Burney, Jr.

Death of a Stripper

People are killing other people in droves in this city. So far in 1979, there have been 109 murders in Atlanta. In 1978, there had been "only" seventy-three murders by this date.

One hundred-and-nine citizens shot, stabbed, and strangled by other citizens.

Sometimes it happens in the nice neighborhoods, and it's page one. But mostly it happens where the sun doesn't shine. The victims wind up no more than statistics in the roundup of brutal crimes in the next morning's newspaper.

Young Hui Griffin, for instance. They called her "Young." She was thirty-two and petite and pretty. She was a native of South Korea. She married an American serviceman, and he brought her to this country.

The couple had a child, a daughter. Later, they divorced. Young Hui Griffin had to go to work to support herself and her child.

She took a daytime job, but that didn't bring in enough money. So she took a nighttime job, too.

She was a dancer at a place called the Purple Onion on Stewart Avenue. I don't need to tell you what kind of dancer.

She danced without her clothes.

Young Hui Griffin needed the money. Young sent her daughter to live with the child's grandmother during the school year. Grandmother lives in the country.

"She didn't want the kid growing up in the city," a friend of Young's explained. "She had to live in a bad neighborhood. She was afraid to leave the kid in her apartment while she worked. She was saving to buy a house so the two of them could be together all the time."

There were also Young's relatives back in South Korea. She was sending as much as $500 a month home so that two brothers and a sister could receive the education she never had.

Young Hui Griffin made the papers this week, inside section, in a roundup story headed, "Four Slayings Boost City's Total to 109."

Police had received a report of her screams. Evidence, said the story, indicated she had staggered into her living room after being stabbed in a bedroom.

So far, there are no suspects.

The man at the Purple Onion this week said he would be glad to talk about Young Hui Griffin.

"She was a damn good person," said Mike Acker, the manager. "You know about how she was trying to help her kid and her relatives, don't you?"

I said I did.

"She was like that. She worked here off and on for three years. She was a good worker. She had a reputation as always being respectful to management.

"She was never late, and if she was going to miss work or something, she would always let you know about it in advance."

I asked Mike Acker about his place, the Purple Onion.

"It used to be a little rough," he said, "but we moved, and we get just about all kinds in here now. We get the men who fly the airplanes, and we get the ones who load 'em. We get construction foremen, and we get construction workers.

"Young danced topless. She would do Oriental dances, like with fans, to basic rock 'n' roll music. A lot of customers really got off on that. She would dance two numbers, and then wait tables.

"Know what else she would do? She was some kind of cook. She was always bringing in things like egg rolls for the other employees to eat. We'll miss that."

There had been some talk around, Mike Acker said, some talk that maybe Young had taken some crazy home with her and that's how she got killed.

"I don't pay any attention to that, though," he said. "What she did after she left this place was none of my business. And we'd probably all be surprised how many working girls leave their regular jobs and turn tricks for money or kicks or whatever."

I'll tell you what else would probably surprise us. To find out those 109 Atlanta murder victims were real people, not faceless, nameless statistics. Real people with hopes and dreams and crosses to bear like the rest of us.

Real people like Young Hui Griffin, a topless dancer who got her throat cut. But she was also mother to a daughter, and a sister who cared to a family who loved her and needed her and, no doubt, hates like hell that she's gone.

A Right to Private Grief

This is when it is hell working for a newspaper.

A young woman is driving home from a party in Cobb County nearly a year ago. She is twenty-five and single, her best years still ahead of her.

She has friends and loving parents. She has a boyfriend.

She never makes it home that night. She disappears with no traces whatsoever. Police can turn up no clues.

And the months and months of grief begin for those close to Nancy Carol Campbell.

The rain was pelting down all over the metro area Wednesday. Most of the talk in the newsroom of The *Constitution* concerned Tuesday's election.

Then, the call came. A car had been found submerged in water alongside the route Nancy Campbell was believed to have taken the night of her disappearance.

Slowly, the details came in. It was Nancy Campbell's car, and she was inside it. Early reports said her death appeared to have been accidental. It's a lousy job, but it has to be done. The softies say, "Leave her family and friends alone. They have enough to bear."

But this is a big city, and this is big city journalism and somebody has to make those calls.

I tried the parents' home first. What would their reaction be? Relief? What were those months and months of no answers like? Another reporter, who had worked on the Nancy Campbell story from the beginning, was with me.

"I don't believe I could do it," she said. "I don't believe I could talk to the parents after what they've been through."

The phone rang at the Campbell home. A woman answered. I identified myself. My hands were shaking.

"I'm sorry," said the woman, "but the Campbells aren't taking any calls. You must understand."

I understood. Frankly, I was relieved.

There were other calls by other reporters. To Colorado, the last known address of John Kurtz, Nancy Campbell's boyfriend. There were calls to an Atlanta friend who has since moved to California. No luck.

I tried a former sorority sister of Nancy Campbell's. She answered. I told her what had happened.

"Oh, my God," said Peggy Reese. "I'm in shock."

We talked maybe fifteen minutes. Peggy Reese, who teaches school, said she had been "very close" to Nancy Campbell, that she had always felt something "bizarre" had happened to her friend.

I asked how they became so close.

"We were at Georgia together," she said, "and I had been in a car accident. My leg was all bandaged up, and I was telling Nancy how bored I was because I wasn't getting to go out.

"Nancy got me a date. We wound up dating these two guys who were friends, and we saw a lot of each other after that."

After Georgia, Peggy Reese and Nancy Campbell stayed in touch. They talked on the telephone, about their lives, about their futures. "I really believe Nancy was a happy person," Peggy Reese said. "She liked her job. She was doing some photography which she enjoyed.

"She and John had been dating a long time, but I don't think she was ready to get married. We are in that age group where we are looking for a lot of things in life."

We talked about Nancy's parents.

"I went to see them several times," Peggy said. "It was awful. They were so down, so depressed. I was convinced they would never breathe another happy breath.

"What happened today will be rough on them right now, but maybe in the long run, it will be better they know."

Later, I thought about trying to call Nancy Campbell's parents again.

I decided not to. To hell with big city journalism on a dreary Wednesday afternoon. People have a right to grieve in private.

Religion and Larry Flynt

It was the prettiest day of late winter. Larry Flynt was somewhere between life and death on an operating table in Button Gwinnett Hospital. Lawrenceville radio station WLAW was on the air with its daily gospel hour.

The first record, the announcer said, was the number one gospel tune in the country, "I'm A Believer Since Jesus Showed Me The Way."

Some nut gunned down Larry Flynt and one of his lawyers on a Lawrenceville street Monday. "Nothing like this has ever happened here before," said an old man at the hospital. Larry Flynt was on trial here for peddling dirty books. Larry Flynt said recently he is a believer since Jesus showed him the way.

Many people don't believe that.

One woman was talking to another woman outside the hospital emergency room.

"I bet the Mafia done it," she said. "He made too much money for the Mafia not to be in on this."

The other woman agreed.

Somebody else said it was probably "some religious fanatic." Larry Flynt gave his views on religion at the trial last week. Some didn't hold to the strictest of Christian doctrine. I remember one of the things he said: "The Bible is a tool to live by, but it shouldn't be an obstacle course."

Flowers were already pouring in for Flynt. There were roses from somebody named Stan Coakley in Killbruck, Ohio. The card read, "Hang in there."

Another arrangement came in from a Bob Flamm. There was no address. The card read, "You showed me how fear can shake a mountain and how faith could move it. Keep the faith. I'm pulling for you all the way."

One of the flower-bearers at the hospital said, "You haven't seen anything. We're making one up from the PTL Club that's gonna be six-foot tall."

PTL stands for "Praise The Lord." The PTL Club is a Christian television program that is shown all over America, Canada and Latin America. Atlantans see it on Channel 36. Its headquarters are in Charlotte. A man named Jim Bakker founded it, runs it and is the television program host.

He sent the flowers.

I couldn't reach Jim Bakker Monday. I talked to his assistant, Robert Manzano, by telephone. Here is what he told me about Larry Flynt and religion:

"Some of our members met Larry Flynt in New York and invited him to Charlotte to talk with Jim Bakker on the PTL Club.

"He came but he was not put on the show. He and Jim Bakker went into another room and talked about religion off the record. Jim was concerned about Mr. Flynt's sincerity concerning his recent conversion.

"The interview was taped, and when it ended, Jim Bakker said he really believed Mr. Flynt was a born-again Christian and that he was honest and sincere.

"He said he was a brandnew Christian and confused and not clear in his philosophy. We caught a lot of flak from religious groups for having anything to do with Larry Flynt at all.

"But Jim Bakker said because he was a new Christian and confused, we needed to love him and help him rather than reject him. He said, 'It is the job of a Christian to love and not to judge.' "

I asked the man to repeat that for me. I wanted to make sure I had it straight.

"It is the job of a Christian," he said, "to love and not to judge."

The woman with the Mafia idea was talking to her friend again.

"You reckon he REALLY got religion?" she asked.

"If he didn't before," her friend said, looking into the emergency room, "I bet he's got it now."

• 11 •

SOME OLD PEOPLE

*Come to think of it, the one burning ambition in my life is to live
long enough to become an old man . . .*

Smokey Bailey

The past few months had been good ones for Ottis "Smokey" Bailey, a friend of mine. Smokey Bailey is the man who collects Bibles and then gives them away to people he thinks "need a good talkin' from the Lord."

I first met him in the cool of a springtime evening as he sat in his favorite chair under some trees behind the big apartment buildings at 2450 Peachtree. Smokey worked there as the building custodian. He lived in the basement.

"I come out here in the evenings," he told me, "to study the Book. Every answer to every question ever been is in the Book."

I wrote a couple of columns about Smokey, and you responded with hundreds of Bibles for him. He beamed each time I brought over a new load.

Later, I would see him on street corners from Buckhead to Brookwood, preaching to anybody who would listen—preaching to anybody.

There was the sweltering day in Buckhead. Smokey, long sleeves and a hat, stood in the park across from the old Capri Theater, Bible held high in one hand, the other hand waving toward the heavens.

He was glad to see me.

"Done give every one of them Bibles away," he said. "Lot of

folks out there got the Word wouldn't have had it if you hadn't brought me them Bibles."

I passed along the credit to those who had taken the time, who had gone to the expense to load Smokey's Biblical arsenal.

Smokey Bailey is nearly sixty. He's a color-blind black man without family, without a purpose other than to do what he thinks the Lord has insisted he do.

For his custodial work at the apartment buildings, he was paid $200 a month. Most of that went for new Bibles. He had layaway accounts at Buckhead book stores. Smokey was always busted, and Wednesday his world caved in.

There are several versions to the story. Aycock, the management company that runs Smokey's building, said Smokey was evicted Wednesday because the building owner, Mrs. Dorothy Johnson, instructed that it be done.

"He wasn't doing his job," said Garvin Aycock. "All I could do was what the law directs me to do."

Mrs. Johnson has refused comment.

A resident who asked that her name not be used ("or I'd be evicted, too") said, "A lot of it was racial. One of the men residents here complained that Smokey put his hand on some of the women's shoulders. He put his hand on my shoulder. And then he'd say, 'God bless you.'

"There wasn't that much work for Smokey to do in the first place. Mrs. Johnson didn't like him preaching either. Whatever else Smokey was, he was harmless. What happened today broke my heart."

Smokey was fired from his job and kicked out on the street. A half-dozen sheriff's deputies came and moved his meager belongings from his basement apartment out to the sidewalk on Peachtree.

Smokey *had* been warned. His checks had been stopped. "I didn't know where else to go," Smokey told me later. "I didn't know they would do me that way. That ain't no way to do anybody."

People from Atlanta's Housing Support Service came to help

Smokey. They hired a truck to move away his belongings. Bibles were scattered up and down the sidewalk. A chair wouldn't fit in the truck. A passerby stopped and purchased it for seven dollars. The movers gave the money to Smokey.

He was eventually taken to the Salvation Army, which has agreed to house him for ten days. Somebody paid to have his few possessions stored.

I can't place any blame here. Maybe Smokey should have spent more time on his custodial duties before heading for his streetside pulpit. And he did have notice that the eviction was coming.

But an old man with a big heart and a message of love is homeless today, and that makes me sick to my stomach.

I do remember something Smokey said to me once, however. It had to do with not being overly concerned with personal gains and security while running in the human race.

"Money ain't never worried me," he said, "'cause my wages are comin' later. The Lord's been holdin' 'em for me."

Pauline Jones

Pauline Jones had enough troubles as it was. She is crippled and in a wheelchair. Arthritis. She was married once, but that was a long time ago. There were no children.

She has two sisters in Atlanta, but they have health problems of their own. They can't help. Pauline is sixty-eight. And she is alone in the city.

What keeps her going is her stubbornness. You need that, and a good measure of it, when you fight The Big Red Tape Machine.

Two months ago, she entered a hospital for surgery on her legs. Doctors say there is a possibility she may even walk again. Pauline is still in the hospital going through a period of rehabilitation.

But it has been slow. Slower than normal because she doesn't know if she will have a place to live when the hospital releases her.

It all began months ago when the Atlanta Housing Authority

ordered her to leave her apartment at the AHA high-rise at 2240 Peachtree.

The other tenants were complaining. Mrs. Jones drinks too much, they said. She gets frightened in the middle of the night and calls the fire department, they said. And she keeps cats in her apartment. There is a rule against pets in AHA apartments.

Pauline wouldn't budge. "Somebody poisoned one of my cats," she says. "I had two kittens left in my apartment. They are all I have."

The AHA took her to court. Tenants from her apartment came by bus to testify. The jury ruled she must leave. Her attorney managed to hold off any further action by appealing to a higher court. Recently, the higher court ruled against Pauline Jones again.

She got that bad news in the hospital the other day from her own law firm, which decided to inform her in a rather matter-of-fact letter that also mentioned she might be evicted within ten days. Pauline didn't need that. "Physically, she is coming along fine," said a doctor at her bedside. "But psychologically, all this hasn't helped a bit."

I talked with two lawyers and one housing authority spokesperson about Pauline Jones this week. "We had no choice," they said. "We had the other tenants to think about. We even offered her another apartment, but she wouldn't take it." Graciously, the AHA says it will not evict Pauline from her apartment until the higher court sends down its final order to the lower court. "Then," said the spokesperson, "we will proceed."

The AHA's suggestion for Pauline Jones is a private nursing home.

I looked to finger a heavy here, but I don't know exactly who it is.

The housing authority is legally within its rights to evict resident Pauline Jones. The other tenants, just as needy, were howling. Fire trucks in the middle of the night aren't exactly what elderly people living in a high-rise apartment building need to see.

And the AHA had offered Pauline another place to live. It had warned her of the consequences if she didn't vacate.

And she *is* stubborn, and she *is* eccentric, but at sixty-eight, she has every right to be.

She doesn't understand how bureaucracies work, and she doesn't understand legalese. And the thought of moving frightened her.

And when it gets lonely in the night, who can begrudge her a drink and a couple of cats to keep her company?

And when she asked me last week, "Where will I go when I leave the hospital? How can I afford a nursing home on $188.40 a month?" I didn't have an answer for her.

It's a big-city dilemma. An urban-living standoff. Nobody to blame. Nobody to go to for help. And a little old lady nobody seems to want is caught squarely in the middle of it all.

The Man With No Socks

He was an old man out of a picture book, and I am a sucker for old men. We would get along famously, I was certain. I would ask questions about the mysteries of life and living and he would provide answers based on the truths experience had taught him.

I watched him totter across the street toward the bus stop in downtown. He wore a tattered baseball cap. If I live long enough to be an old man, I will wear a tattered baseball cap.

His shirt was wrinkled. His pants were baggy. There were no strings in his shoes and he wore no socks. Why, on such a fine spring morning, should a man have to lace his shoes and wear socks if he chooses not to?

He carried a newspaper under his arm. He shaved sometime last week. If I live long enough to be an old man, I will browse over the newspaper at my leisure in the mornings and shave only when I damn well please.

He peered at the first bus that came by and chose not to board it. He asked the obnoxious dude standing next to him had such-and-such bus been by. He got no reply. The young tough ignored the old man. The young tough also wore an ear ornament. Never trust or strike up conversations with men who decorate their ears.

It was my chance to talk to the old man.

"Need any help?" I asked.

"Help?" he asked back. "I don't need any help. I need a bus. I ain't stayin' down here all day."

I apologized. Old men can be stubborn and independent. If I live long enough to be an old man, I will be stubborn and independent and defy anybody to treat me like an old man.

"I came down here to get my check," he went on. "The government gives me enough to live on. I don't need much. I don't smoke. I don't drink. I used to drink, but I don't drink anymore. And I don't fool with no women. That's what costs money, foolin' with women."

I was pressing my luck, I knew, but I wanted to keep the conversation going.

I asked if he had any family.

"I had a wife," he said. "she's been dead thirty-five years."

And children?

"A houseful. That's why I never did marry again. You get that many young'uns to raise, you ain't got no time to be out chasin' around for another wife."

A bus came by. He squinted through the morning sun and tried to see the sign above the front window. It wasn't his bus. I was glad. I wanted to hear more.

"You believe I'm eighty-one years old?" he asked me.

He looked every day of it, but I lied. I told him I couldn't believe he was eighty-one.

"Well, I'm not," he laughed. "I'm just eighty. But if the Lord lets me live another month, I'll be eighty-one."

He was rolling now, the old man. He talked about his children. Some were successful. One son had a house with eight rooms in it. Some were not so successful. He had a daughter who had been in a wreck.

"Drinkin' caused it," he said. "She had $35,000 worth of doctor bills. I told her to quit the bottle. She wouldn't listen to me. I knew something bad was going to happen to her, and it did."

He had another daughter drinking bad, too, he said. The old man said he went to her house last week and gave her $37 and some food stamps and then went back later and found her and her husband at the kitchen table drinking beer.

"I'm through with 'em now," he said. "I tried one time to get 'em to come live with me, but they won't. You know why?"

I didn't have the slightest.

" 'Cause every morning I get me some good preachin' and some good gospel singin' on the radio, and they don't want to listen to that," he said. "I guess they're afraid it might do 'em some good."

His bus finally arrived. We shook hands and he was gone in a cloud of MARTA fumes. If I live long enough to be an old man, I'll play my preachin' and singin' as long and as loud as I please and the devil with any of my ungrateful children who don't have the good sense to listen to it.

Invitation

The speeding Metroliner from Washington to New York last week had already passed through Baltimore and its railside ghetto that seems to stretch into an endless prairie of shacks from the window of the train.

Wilmington would be next. Then Philadelphia, and on to Trenton, through the ruins of Newark, and into the tunnel that leads to Pennsylvania Station.

I had seen all this before. I know every junkyard by heart. This is one train ride where the scenery is a liability to those who would espouse the benefits of downtown-to-downtown rail travel.

I do not want to be accused of provincial prejudice. I sat next to a man from New Jersey on this same trip once. I'll let him describe the view traveling by train up the eastern seaboard:

"One big dump," is how he put it.

You look for diversions on a trip like this. A newspaper will last you barely past Capital Beltway, the first stop out of Washington. I like to pass the time talking to people who will talk back.

Like the old man who sat down beside me out of Baltimore and ordered up a cup of coffee, cream and sugar. One gulp into his refreshment and he was gushing with conversation.

A lot of people won't listen to old men. A lot of people are stupid.

His clothes were wrinkled and tired, but he had at least bothered to wear what was left of his tie. There was a dignity about him. When he talked, his blue eyes danced about. His hair was solid in post-gray white. He was a little man, but not stooped.

"Goin' to New York, sir?" he asked me. I said I was. He said he was, too. The traveler's ice was broken. Imagine, I thought to myself, this old man addressing me as "sir."

"I'm seeing the ball game today at Yankee Stadium," he continued. "I live in Baltimore, but I go to see the Yankees. The Orioles have no team, no team at all. Now, the Yankees, there is a team."

I used to talk a lot of baseball with my grandfather. He barely got out of Heard County, Georgia, in his seventy-three years, but he knew some baseball.

"Do you know, sir," the old man went on, "I saw Mr. George Herman Ruth hit his first home run in Yankee Stadium? That was fifty-six years ago. Nineteen-and-twenty-three.

"They talk about ball players today. There are no ball players today like we used to have ball players. Ever hear of Mr. Ty Cobb, sir?"

I said I had heard of him.

"Hit three-sixty-something lifetime. LIFETIME! Can you imagine somebody hittin' three-sixty-something lifetime today?"

He took another gulp of the coffee.

"Did you know, sir, Mr. George Herman Ruth was also a pitcher? He was also one fine pitcher. Held some records for shutout innings in the World Series. He was the greatest ball player of all time. I saw him hit his first home run in Yankee Stadium in Nineteen-and-twenty-three."

If I had seen something like that, I would repeat myself, too.

"I know all about the Yankees," the old man said. We were coming into Wilmington. "I could name you the starting lineup of the 1923 Yankees, sir, do you believe I could do that?"

I didn't have time to answer. He was already off and naming. Few of the names meant anything to me, but his feat was impressive, nevertheless. I can name the starting lineup of the 1959 Dodgers and White Sox. It didn't seem worth bringing up, however.

Philadelphia was next. When they finally close Thirtieth Street Station in Philadelphia, they can use it for a dungeon. Trenton. Then, Newark. I would hate to live in Newark.

Five minutes into the tunnel that leads to New York, the conductor announced Pennsylvania Station. The old man was still talking. Among other things, he predicted the Yankees would win the World Series again because Tommy John keeps his pitches low.

"You're a busy man?" he asked me. Very, I said.

Later, after he had tottered away, and I had departed the station for a task that wasn't all that important in retrospect, I concluded the old man had probably considered asking me if I wanted to go to the ball game at Yankee Stadium with him. But I was too busy, I had said. A lot of people are stupid.

Barney

Barney Wisdom is dead. It happened Monday. Everybody has a right to an obituary, I was thinking. Even old winos. This is Barney's. It's the least I can do.

It won't be that complete, however, because nobody knew much about Barney—and he could barely talk—except he was a pitiful sight hobbling around the Howell Mill-Collier Road area in Northwest Atlanta looking for his next drink.

"I'm not that sad Barney died," a lady from the neighborhood told me. "It's probably a blessing. It just breaks my heart he had to live the way he did."

Barney was sixty-nine. A policeman found that out. Somebody said he was a native of Alabama and used to work in a sawmill. Somebody else said he had a son in Florence. There was talk he might have a sister in Summerville in north Georgia, and I even heard once he had a brother over in Lawrenceville.

A man at the coroner's office told me Wednesday he had tried to contact a relative to claim Barney's body from the Grady morgue.

"So far," he said, "nothing."

Barney was the *quintessential* wino. He worked at it all his waking hours. His favorite drinking perch was atop a bench on the side of Springlake Pharmacy at the corner of Howell Mill and Collier.

Barney never bothered anybody that I knew of. Give him a buck and he would return a toothless smile that was certainly not without charm. Barney was the subject of another column of mine a few months back.

Two rascal children were throwing rocks at him as he sat beside the drugstore one Saturday afternoon. I wrote about the incident in the newspaper. I heard the two children moved out of town. Good riddance.

Barney slept in the woods off Howell Mill. Or in the basement of a neighborhood laundromat. Or, when the weather became unbearable, down at Atlanta's Union Mission, thanks to rides by caring Atlanta policemen.

That's where he died. A passing motorist found him nearly comatose on the sidewalk Monday afternoon. Barney had been fading fast lately. A few months back, there was even a rumor he had died, but Barney showed up again, thirsty as ever.

The motorist took him to the Union Mission. One of the spokesmen there told me what happened:

"Barney was in bad shape," he said. "The first thing we do is give them a shower and then find some clean clothes. We gave him the shower, and then he just fell over dead."

He was taken to the Grady morgue. Police investigated and did find Barney had a small bank account.

"I believe he has enough to bury him," explained a teller at the bank. "I hope so. He didn't have a very good life. I would at least like to see him put away nicely."

The alternative, of course, is a pauper's funeral at county expense.

I live in the Howell-Collier area, and I always marveled at the special—and surprising—interest the neighborhood had in Barney, the old boozer who was as much a local landmark as Springlake Pharmacy, home of the world's finest limeade coolers.

I made a speech to the local Garden Club last week. After the speech, I asked for questions:

"How's Barney?" was the first response from a little, gray lady.

Capital City Liquor store is across the street from Springlake Pharmacy. Needless to say, Barney spent a great deal of time there.

"We cashed his social security checks," said one of the men there. "Barney didn't beg when he was out of money. He'd just stand there and look at you.

"He could wear you down physchologically. I wish I had a nickel for every fifty cents he got from me."

I hope some of Barney's relatives—if there are any—read this, and I hope they show enough interest to make sure one of his own is standing by when shovels of dirt cover his last remains.

Everybody has a right to blood kin at his funeral, I was thinking. Even old winos.